The Total Money Makeover
WORKBOOK

Other Books by Dave Ramsey

The Total Money Makeover

Financial Peace

Financial Peace Revisited

Financial Peace Planner

Financial Peace for the Next Generation (Youth Book)

Tranquilidad Financiera (Spanish edition of *Financial Peace*)

More Than Enough

More Than Enough Planner

The Super Red Racer (Children's Book)

Priceless (Four-Color Gift Book)

The Total Money Makeover
WORKBOOK

A Proven Plan for Financial Fitness

Dave Ramsey

THOMAS NELSON
Since 1798

NASHVILLE   DALLAS   MEXICO CITY   RIO DE JANEIRO   BEIJING

Published in Nashville, Tennessee, by Thomas Nelson, Inc.

Scripture quotations are from THE NEW KING JAMES VERSION, Copyright © 1979, 1980, 1982, Thomas Nelson, Inc., Publishers.

ISBN 13: 978-0-7852-6327-2
ISBN 10: 0-7852-6327-6

Printed in the United States of America

08 09 10 VG 24

Contents

1

The Total Money
Makeover Challenge

Key Concept #1

No Money . . . Is No Fun

I remember the feelings vividly. For several years in my twenties, I faced the end of every month with dread. I had too much month left at the end of my money. I was not having fun.

I wasn't afraid of hard work and sacrifice. I didn't need a secret formula for making money. I didn't need a positive-thinking guru to pump me up and tell me to have a positive attitude. I was simply sick and tired of being sick and tired when it came time to "do the bills." I felt hopeless, as if I were running a financial race with no traction and no ground covered. Money came in and money went out, with nothing REAL to show for my effort or income.

What About You?

Do you feel as if you have full control over your money . . . or are your bills controlling you? The amount of control you have over financial matters is often reflected in how you FEEL about money matters in general.

The same thing is true, of course, when it comes to any area of your life in which a "makeover" might be needed.

If you are in very bad health—or your physician tells you that certain numbers in your lab reports and exams are "abnormal"—you may become highly motivated to undertake a new exercise, diet, or better-health plan. If your spouse tells you the end of your marriage is on the horizon—you may become highly motivated to seek out a counselor to help you revamp the way you relate to your spouse and to improve your marriage. There's a feeling that hits the pit of your stomach when you finally wake up and say to yourself, "Something's got to change! I can't continue to live this way . . . the fact is, to continue this way isn't really to LIVE. It's just to exist, to endure, to put in the time and the miles and hope I end up somewhere I like."

Before you are truly willing to embark on a Total Money Makeover, you need to face up to how you FEEL about your current financial situation. That will tell you how motivated you are to do something about changing your financial situation.

Plain and simple, if you like your current financial situation, you probably feel pretty good about money matters, and you don't need a makeover.

On the other hand, if you DON'T like your current financial situation, you probably feel pretty lousy about your finances. A makeover is for you!

Exercise #1

How Do You Feel About Money?

I challenge you to take the "Ten Situations Test" below.

Respond to each of the statements below quickly and instinctively with a simple "I like to talk about this" or "I don't like to discuss this."

LIKE to Talk: The "LIKE to Talk" category includes responses such as "I enjoy getting new ideas about this" and "I don't have anything to hide on this subject."

"LIKE to talk" should reflect an enthusiasm—not a reluctance—for talking, and a willingness to be open, honest, and candid. Finally, the "LIKE to talk" category should not reflect just an "I've got a pat answer already prepared" attitude, but rather an "I think this is a good opportunity for a candid sharing of ideas and opinions" attitude.

HATE to Talk: Included in the "HATE to talk" category are responses such as "I wouldn't be caught dead discussing this" and "I'd do just about anything to avoid a serious conversation about this." "HATE to Talk" should be checked if you feel reluctance, awkwardness, or dread.

LIKE to Talk	HATE to Talk	
❑	❑	1. Someone asks, "How are you doing financially?"
❑	❑	2. Your spouse wants to discuss this month's budget.
❑	❑	3. Your tax accountant calls and says, "Let's meet."
❑	❑	4. Your pastor wants to have lunch with you (and you know he wants to discuss the possibility of your making a specific contribution).
❑	❑	5. Your child asks you to co-sign a loan (or a credit-card application).
❑	❑	6. The money manager in your family says, "I have some concerns about a few credit-card charges."
❑	❑	7. A friend says, "What do you invest your money in?"
❑	❑	8. A supplier or vendor asks, "Do you want this automatically deducted from your bank account each month?"
❑	❑	9. A loan officer says, "Tell me about your financial situation."
❑	❑	10. A parent asks, "Did you ever pay off that debt you had?"

Most thin, fit people ENJOY telling those who ask about their exercise routine, the diet plan that helped them shed the pounds, and other health matters. Thin, fit people are actually MORE likely to see a physician or read health-related articles than those who are overweight or out of shape.

Those who have children who are excelling, or who have marriages that are loving, usually ENJOY talking about their family relationships.

And . . . those who are financially fit usually ENJOY talking about money matters and sharing their insights into money management.

Take another look at the way you responded to the situations listed above. Overall, how do you rate your willingness to face and discuss your financial situations?

Circle one of the two responses below . . . and then cross through the statement that does NOT reflect the way you feel:

Response #1: Overall, I am WILLING and EAGER to discuss financial matters openly and candidly.

Response #2: Overall, I am NOT WILLING and NOT EAGER to discuss financial matters openly and candidly.

Exercise #2

Scared or Smiling?

How do you FEEL—gut-level, first response—about each of the twelve money matters below, on a scale of 1 to 4 (1 being "scared" and 4 being "Smiling All the Way")?

(1)	(2)	(3)	(4)
Scared	**A Little Worried**	**Under Control**	**Smiling All the Way**

1. Paying this month's utility bills: _____

2. Making the current car payment: _____

3. Paying next month's mortgage: _____

4. Funding retirement: _____

5. Paying for the kids' college: _____

6. Paying back a loan: _____

7. Paying the minimum on this month's credit-card bills: _____

8. Paying off all this month's credit-card bills in full: _____

9. Ability to handle an emergency expense: _____

10. Prepared to pay for a child's wedding: _____

11. Having your children think well of you because of the inheritance you will leave to them when you die: _____

12. Taking a nice family vacation this year: _____

The truth of the matter is . . .

If you feel SCARED or fearful about any of these money matters, you likely are NOT in control of your finances—they are running your life, and perhaps even ruining your life!

If you feel A LITTLE WORRIED, you also are NOT in control of your finances—you very likely just aren't admitting how scared or fearful you are that things could spin out of control at any moment. Those who are A LITTLE WORRIED are only "a little confident" that things are going in the right direction.

If you feel UNDER CONTROL, you may very well BE in control . . . or you may be in a state of denial about your finances. I have encountered numerous people who say, "No problem," because that's the way they want their lives to be, when in truth, anybody looking objectively at their situation would shout out loud, "Man, you've got a PROBLEM!" *Control* is a term we sometimes use to talk ourselves into believing that things are going to turn out all right, and that a negative situation is manageable—a little like riding a bucking bronco is manageable if you manage to stay in the saddle.

SMILING ALL THE WAY . . . should be interpreted as "smiling all the way TO THE

BANK AND BACK"! If you checked "smiling" for most of these statements, it's likely you don't need a TOTAL Money Makeover. But . . . you may need money makeover tips for those specific areas in which you answered anything other than SMILING ALL THE WAY.

Key Concept #2
If You Don't Know How Money Works . . .
What Future Is There in Working for Money?

When I was in my late twenties, my wife and I went broke. We lost everything because I didn't know how money works. We hit bottom hard and lost everything. It was then I began a serious quest to learn how money works. I came to realize:

1. *It's up to me.* My money problems, worries, and shortages largely began and ended in my mirror—nobody "made" me poor or a bad money manager. I had to take full responsibility for my own stupidity.

2. *God's and Grandma's way of handling money works.* Wealth building isn't rocket science. The principles are simple, time-proven, and effective. In a nutshell, "spend less and invest more" is a five-word financial strategy that every person over the age of five can comprehend!

3. *Winning at money is 80 percent behavior and 20 percent head knowledge.* It's not enough to know good financial principles—it's *acting* on those principles that's important.

What About You?

One of the first things any fitness adviser will tell a person is this: Stand in front of a mirror and take a long, hard look at yourself—preferably while you are wearing minimal clothing. Do you *like* what you see?

If not, are you willing to own up to the fact that YOU are the person who allowed yourself to get fat and flabby?

Are you willing to own up to the fact that the three basic principles of fitness aren't all that difficult to comprehend? Eat less, eat the right foods, and exercise more are concepts even a child can understand.

Are you willing to own up to the fact that it doesn't matter how much you KNOW about diet plans, good nutrition, or exercise UNLESS you are willing to put what you know into high gear? You won't get fit unless you actually EAT right, EAT less, and EXERCISE more.

These are givens in achieving physical fitness.

The same is true for financial fitness.

Exercise #3

Whose Fault Is it?

Check true or false for each of the statements below.

TRUE FALSE

❑   ❑   1. My money problems aren't my fault

❑   ❑   2. My money problems are only PARTLY my fault.

❑   ❑   3. My money problems are MY fault.

If you checked TRUE for statement number one or number two above, you need a reality check. The TRUTH is, your money problems are YOUR fault.

"But . . . ," you may say, "it ISN'T solely my fault." Let's explore that. Whom do you blame for your money problems?

Check any of the following that you believe apply . . . and then tell why.

	My Money Problems Are the Fault of . . .	**MY PART in This Was . . .**
My spouse	❑	_____
My parents	❑	_____
My children	❑	_____

	My Money Problems Are the Fault of . . .	MY PART in This Was . . .
My "bad luck"	❏	_____
Interest rates	❏	_____
My employer	❏	_____
The government	❏	_____
My bank	❏	_____
My financial adviser	❏	_____
My personality type	❏	_____
A bad loan	❏	_____
My stockbroker	❏	_____
The stock market	❏	_____
Other:	❏	_____

Why did YOU allow that person to give you money problems? Your "bad loan" was a loan YOU took out or YOU issued to another person. Right? Your spouse's overspending occurred because YOU agreed to let overspending go unchecked. Right? For any items above that you checked, be honest in completing the following:

	My Money Problems Are the Fault of . . .	MY PART in This Was . . .
My spouse	❏	_____
My parents	❏	_____
My children	❏	_____
My "bad luck"	❏	_____
Interest rates	❏	_____
My employer	❏	_____
The government	❏	_____
My bank	❏	_____

My Money Problems Are the Fault of . . .		MY PART in This Was . . .
My financial adviser	❑	_____
My personality type	❑	_____
A bad loan	❑	_____
My stockbroker	❑	_____
The stock market	❑	_____
Other:	❑	_____

Why am I being so tough with you on this point? Two reasons:

Reason #1: Until you take responsibility for your money situation, you aren't going to do anything to CHANGE because you don't think you CAN do anything. You'll wait for the "other party" to take responsibility, or you'll wait for your luck, stockbroker, or personality to change!

Reason #2: The way you ALLOWED another person or entity to impact your financial situation very often gives good clues about what you need to "undo" as you seek to become financially fit.

Think for a moment about physical fitness. If you are blaming too much ice cream and Mexican food for your excess weight . . . there are clues in your laying blame! You have a weakness when it comes to ice cream and Mexican food. The solution for your problem? Well, in part it's this: Don't bring ice cream home from the supermarket, and don't go out to eat at Mexican restaurants!

At the same time, own up to the fact that YOU are the one who turns your car into the ice cream parlor's parking lot, and YOU are the one who is quick to say, "Let's eat Mexican tonight." You aren't fat because there's a great ice cream store less than a half mile from your home or a Mexican restaurant just around the corner. You'd find a way to overeat or eat the wrong foods, even if all ice cream and all Mexican food disappeared from the planet tomorrow!

Ditto for your money problems. If you are blaming another person or situation for your money problems, you are in denial. The problems are YOURS. Own up to your responsibility in creating money problems for yourself, and then you can do something to turn those problems into solutions.

Exercise #4

The Person in Your Mirror

Check all the statements below that you believe apply to your financial situation:

**This Applies
to Me**

- ❑   1. I don't know enough about how money works.
- ❑   2. I struggle with my bills because of my own poor choices.
- ❑   3. I am the number one person responsible for turning around my financial situation.
- ❑   4. I know what to do with money . . . I just don't do it.
- ❑   5. I haven't ever REALLY taken responsibility for learning how money works.
- ❑   6. I have been lazy when it comes to disciplining myself about money.
- ❑   7. I am willing to take FULL responsibility for my current money situation.
- ❑   8. I am willing to make the changes necessary to enjoy success with my money.

If you checked any of the above, you need a financial makeover—and you know it. Congratulations! You have taken the first REALITY-CHECK step toward improving your handling of money.

Key Concept #3
Take a Short, Painful Walk into a Lifetime of Success

This *Total Money Makeover Workbook* is based on one very simple motto:

> If you will live like no one else NOW . . .
> LATER you can live like no one else.

Living like no one else NOW means living a sacrificial, highly focused, purpose-driven life when it comes to your money.

Living like no one else LATER means living without the worry, frustration, stress, or fear that comes from constantly being on the brink of financial disaster. It means living LATER with feelings of confidence, hope, and joy related to money.

What About You?

Are you willing to change YOU? Honestly?

There are countless millions of people who look in the mirror and believe they SHOULD become more fit. Many of these people will say, "Yes, I NEED to change. I'd LIKE to change." But when it comes right down to changing, they DON'T change. Why? The foremost reason is because they don't like change—period. They don't want to alter any aspect of their lives. They see change as difficult to impossible or, at the very least, uncomfortable.

I agree. Change always has an element of sacrifice to it. It always has an element of self-denial. Any change that truly results in growth or improvement has an element of pain associated with it.

So let me ask again: Are you willing to change YOU?

Exercise #5

The Willingness to Change

In each pair of opposite statements, circle the one that most clearly represents you in ALL areas of your life.

I like change.	I hate change.
I'm willing to learn.	I'm not willing to learn.
I'm willing to adjust my habits if it means a better life.	I like my habits, and I don't believe I'll have to change any of them.
I'm capable of changing.	I don't think I can change.
I am capable of enduring some pain, difficulty, and sacrifice if the goal is worth it.	I'm truly not willing to experience ANY pain, difficulty, or sacrifice.
I can deny myself certain "pleasures" now for long-term pleasure later.	I'm not into denial of any kind.
I am willing to do without some things now in order to have the life I truly want later.	I'm not willing to give up anything I currently have or routinely experience.
I'd rather have the pain of change than have the pain of money problems.	I'd rather live with the pain of money problems than experience the pain of change.

Take a long, hard look at your answers above. If you aren't willing to make some painful changes in your life for the short-run . . . there's no reason to continue on in this book. I suggest you stop reading and then come back to this workbook when the pain of your current financial situation becomes unbearable or you've reached the point that you ARE willing to trade in the pain of money problems for the pain of change. It's only as you are willing to CHANGE that a money makeover will work for you.

Complete the motto if you can:

I am willing to live NOW like _____ one else . . .
so I can live LATER like _____ one else!

Simple Q & A

Q: According to *USA Today*, _____ percent of bankruptcy filers blame credit-card bills for their bankruptcy.

A: 63

Exercise #6

Taking Charge

Fill in the blanks in the seven sentences below. Use the Word Pool if you need help!

1. My financial life will begin turning around when I take full _____ for the money problems I have.

2. I know I'm smart enough to learn how _____ works.

3. I know I am capable of making the _____ necessary to get rid of my money problems and worries.

4. I am _____ to live like no one else NOW in order to live like no one else later.

5. I'd rather be SMILING than _____ when I think about paying bills.

6. I want to be in _____ of my money, rather than have my money _____ me.

7. If it's going to be, it's up to _____ !

Word Pool

money • willing • me • scared • control • responsibility • changes • control

Answers:

1. responsibility

2. money

3. changes

4. willing

5. scared

6. control; control

7. me

Go back and read aloud each of the statements with the correct words filling the blanks!

I'm Not *That* Out of Shape:
DENIAL

Key Concept #1
Most People Are NOT As Well Off as They Think They Are

For years I've conducted live financial seminars in which I've relayed this fact cited in the *Wall Street Journal:*

Seventy percent of Americans live paycheck to paycheck.

This statistic, of course, means that only 30 percent of Americans DON'T live paycheck to paycheck. Fewer than one out of three of us have SOMETHING set aside to allow us NOT to face a money problem if we miss ONE paycheck.

Simple Q & A

Q: According to *USA Today,* _____ percent of bankruptcy filers still get offers for new credit cards!

A: 89

It amazes me that when I ask an audience at the start of a seminar, "Are you in the 70 percent group or the 30 percent group?" . . . the majority of the people say they are in the 30 percent group. By the end of the day, the vast majority are willing to admit the truth: They are in the 70 percent group.

What About You?

The mirror very rarely lies when it comes to physical fitness and health. MOST physical problems are evident—if not immediately, eventually. Even if a person isn't grossly overweight, he or she can be "flabby." And even if a person isn't overweight or flabby, he or she still can be "unfit," which will show up in wrinkles on the face, skin tone, the condition of hair and nails, stooped-over posture, dark circles under the eyes, a pale or "in pain" countenance, a general lack of "looking well," and so forth. Poor fitness and poor health are hard to camouflage, even with expensive makeup.

On the other hand, good physical fitness is evident. The physically fit person has a sparkle in his eyes, a bounce in his step, a glow to his face, a relaxed demeanor that is, at the same time, ready to burst with energy.

Sadly, financial fitness is far LESS evident. Many people have fooled themselves into thinking they are much more fit than they actually are.

Exercise #7

A Starting Point

Just for fun, mark on the scale below where you think YOU are when it comes to financial FITNESS:

Very Fit	**Moderately Fit**	**Somewhat Fit**	**Not Very Fit**	**NOT FIT!**

And now . . . let's check that estimate.

Case Study: Sara and John

Sara and John had a combined family income of $75,000 a year. They had the so-called "normal" debts of many couples in their age and income ranges: a small student loan, a car loan, and about $5,000 on a credit card. They had virtually no savings—just a few hundred dollars in a second interest-bearing checking account that they called a "savings account." Nonetheless, Sara and John told themselves they were doing well—in fact, they told themselves they were really on top of things financially. So, they decided to build a new house.

Both John and Sara later admitted to having a few "uneasy" feelings about building a new and larger house, but they figured they were experiencing "normal jitters," and they forged ahead. They moved into their new house in May, and then in September, Sara was called into a meeting with her boss. She was expecting a promotion and raise for the good work she had done. Instead, she learned that her company was "downsizing," and she was out of a job!

In one day, the family income went from $75,000 to $45,000. By the end of the day, not only was Sara reeling from feelings of rejection and a wounded pride, she was feeling the tentacles of financial failure creeping toward her and her family. She and John sat down with their budget, and they didn't like what they saw as a new bottom line. They went to bed that night aware that foreclosure on their new house might be a reality in the near future.

Sara told me, "We took a long, hard look in the financial mirror, and we saw 'fat' people who were terribly out of shape financially. We knew we had to cut back dramatically and immediately if we were going to survive for even a few weeks without my income."

Motivated to a great extent by feelings of sheer panic, Sara shifted into high gear in her search for a new job, and, fortunately, she was able to find a position and embark on an entirely new career path in about a month. She said, "I knew I was one of the lucky ones. Some of the others who were downsized didn't find jobs for four, six, even nine months."

The feelings of panic for Sara didn't disappear with the new job. She and John talked at length about their financial goals, and Sara admitted to John that she never wanted to feel such panic and dread again. She said, "I didn't feel the least bit exhilarated at the 'risk' of not having a job. I felt more vulnerable and nervous than ever in my life. I told John I didn't ever want to have those feelings again. I feel very fortunate that John understood my feelings and didn't criticize me for them. I told him I was willing to make any sacrifices we had to make in the next several years if it meant achieving some level of financial security."

The most important change for Sara and John came when they decided that they would seek to live at a financial level that *required* only one income, not two. They mutually agreed to cut back their spending and work at paying off their loans. Their goal was to NEED only HALF of their combined family income for basic living expenses. They decided the other "half" would be money they would invest in retirement or use for an occasional trip or luxury. They also decided they would live on a cash basis, without credit cards or loans other than the house mortgage.

It took Sara and John a little over two years to get to the point where they had paid off the school loan, the credit cards, and the car loan, and they had put some money away in an "emergency" fund. They decided the emergency fund needed to include an amount of money that reflected three months of their "expenses." Their reasoning was that surely the person who had lost a job would be able to find another job in three months.

Sara and John currently have *only* their house mortgage as an outstanding debt. Overall, their monthly bills have been reduced by about 40 percent. Meanwhile, John has received a raise, and so has Sara. They are paying down the principal of their mortgage to reduce their monthly payments. As they stand right now, they are within a year of having their monthly bills balanced against their income so they *could* live on HALF their combined family income.

Are Sara and John excited about their progress? Absolutely. Sara said with a great deal of confidence, "We know where we are, we know where we are going, and we know how we are going to get there. We are no longer living in denial about where we are financially. We *know*. We are no longer living the lie we were living when I lost my job—the lie that 'everything is just fine.' Today, when I say, 'Things are fine,' they really *are* fine. And they are fine because we faced reality, made some drastic decisions, and worked very hard to change our financial situation so we are at a level that is both comfortable and realistic."

Exercise #8

Let's Get Real

This exercise is long, and I admit to you that it may seem a little complicated as you work through it. (Some people don't like dealing with math.) I recommend you grab a calculator. The exercise will help you see how much at risk you are if just one wage earner in your family loses his or her job.

How much money do you make a month
(combined family income)? $ _____

How much of this each month do you save or
put in an investment account that you can
access and that isn't at risk (such as a money-
market fund)? $ _____

Subtract the "savings" amount above from
your total monthly family income to get . . .
NET AVAILABLE CASH FOR PAYING "BILLS"
AND MAKING CHARITABLE CONTRIBUTIONS
EACH MONTH: $ _____

RIGHT NOW . . . how much do you have in a
savings account or in a readily accessible
money fund? $ _____

How much do you have in your checking
account (or WILL have at the end of this
month after all monthly bills are paid)? $ _____

Add these two numbers together to get . . .
TOTAL "READY CASH" AVAILABLE FOR AN
EMERGENCY: $ _____

What percentage of your monthly "spending"
amount does this last number reflect?   _____ percent
(For example: If you have $2,000 in a
savings or money market account . . . and you
have a "net" spending budget of $3,500 a
month, your percentage is 57.
[$2,000 ÷ $3,500 = 57.1428571])

The percentage number represents the "amount" of any given month that you can
"survive" without serious changes in your spending habits should you suddenly
have NO income. In our sample above, 57 percent represents 17 days—or two and
a half weeks (.57 x 30-day month = 17).

How many days can you "live" without any
significant changes to your current lifestyle? _____ days

If your total family income includes income from two or more people—such as
husband and wife—ask yourself . . .

How much of our combined income comes
from Person A? $ _____

How much of our combined income comes
from Person B? $ _____

How much of our combined income comes
from Person C (perhaps an adult child or elderly
parent contributing to family expenses)? $ _____

Total Family Income: $ _____

The total of the three numbers should be the same as the dollar figure you entered
for the first question in this exercise: "How much money do you make a month
(combined family income)?"

Now let's figure out what would happen if you lost the income from one or more
people.

Take the amount of income from Person A and divide it by the total family
income. This gives you the percentage Person A contributes to the total family
income. (For example, if Person A contributes $1,200 to the total family income of
$3,500, divide 1,200 by 3,500 to get 34 percent.)

Percentage contributed by Person A: _____

Then take the amount of income from Person B and divide it by the total family income. This gives you the percentage Person B contributes to the total family income. (For example, if Person B contributes $2,200 to the total family income of $3,500, divide 2,200 by 3,500 to get 63 percent.)

Percentage contributed by Person B: _____

Then take the amount of income from Person C and divide it by the total family income. This gives you the percentage Person C contributes to the total family income. (For example, if Person C contributes $100 to the total family income of $3,500, divide 100 by 3,500 to get 3 percent.)

Percentage contributed by Person C: _____

The three percentage numbers should total 100 percent.
(In our example, 34 + 63 + 3 = 100.)

Now for the serious realization . . .

How many days did you calculate you could live without making any significant changes to your lifestyle (previous set of calculations)? _____ days
Multiply that number by the percentage for each person:

Person A: _____ days x ____ percent = _____ days

Person B: _____ days x ____ percent = _____ days

Person C: _____ days x ____ percent = _____ days

Subtract these days from the total days:

Person A: _____ total days − _____ (number of days above) = _____ days

Person B: _____ total days − _____ (number of days above) = _____ days

Person C: _____ total days − _____ (number of days above) = _____ days

In our example:

If Person A loses his job, which reflects 34 percent of the family income, then this person's income represents 6 days of living expenses. The total of 17 days minus the 6 days "lost" if this income vanishes is 11 days.

If Person B loses her job, which reflects 63 percent of the family income, then this person's income represents 11 days of living expenses. The total of 17 days minus the 11 days "lost" if this income vanishes is 6 days.

If Person C cannot contribute his 3 percent of the family income, this person's absence represents about a half day of income. The total of 17 days minus a half day . . . well, the family can probably survive with a very small adjustment.

What's your story?

If one or more people in your family suddenly couldn't contribute to the total family income . . . How comfortable do you feel about your financial situation?

Exercise #9

What Would Happen If . . .

One of the best ways I know to help a person see his or her financial state for what it really IS, is to ask these five basic questions. I challenge you to take the test! Circle ALL answers that may apply to any one question.

1. What would happen if you lost your job today? What would happen if you were laid off—with no warning—and found yourself out on the streets with your personal possessions by five o'clock? How long could you live your present lifestyle in your present home before you HAD to have another job at the same level of income as your present job?

   a. two weeks
   b. one month
   c. two months
   d. three months
   e. six months or longer

2. What would happen if a physician told you today that you needed to have a serious operation that would require two months of recuperation (NO work) and another month or two of only part-time work before you could resume "full activity"?

   a. I'd lose my job if I had to be away for that long.
   b. I'd likely keep my job but would be forced to take some unpaid "leave" (after sick days and paid vacation days were used up).
   c. I'd keep my job and would be paid for all the time I was away.
   d. I'd refuse the operation because I know I couldn't get another job quickly enough to make ends meet . . . or because I know that it would be very difficult to get another job with that "medical history" hanging around my neck.
   e. I'd quit my job and get well and then regroup and decide what I want to do with the rest of my life . . . and along the way, I wouldn't have any money worries.

3. What would happen if your spouse was in a serious automobile accident today and lost his or her job as a result of a long-term recovery or permanent disability?

a. Everything in our lives would be turned upside down—not just our daily routine, but our finances.

b. We'd be forced to move from our present home.

c. We'd have serious trouble paying more than one month's utility and other regular "bills."

d. We'd have to borrow money if we wanted to maintain our present lifestyle.

e. We'd focus all our energies on my spouse's recovery, without financial worries.

4. What would happen if your supervisor came to you today and said, "The company is downsizing, and you are being offered early retirement . . . And, by the way, if you don't take early retirement, you'll likely be let go"?

a. I'd take early retirement and start doing what I've always wanted to do with my creative energy and time.

b. I'd panic. I need FULL-TIME employment to pay for the things I've purchased on time—"retirement" pay just wouldn't be enough right now.

c. I'd beg and plead to keep my job because without it, I'd have serious and immediate money problems.

d. It wouldn't matter how much severance they gave me, I'd need to get another job within a couple of months or I'd have to move from my current residence.

5. What would happen if an elderly parent had to move in with you (because there was no other place for that parent to go), which would require you to quit your part-time job and rely solely on your spouse's full-time job?

a. We'd have to stop all luxuries in our life.

b. We wouldn't be able to continue to pay for our child's college tuition.

c. We'd probably have to trade in my luxury car for a lesser vehicle.

d. We'd have to rethink just about everything in our budget.

e. We'd make it just fine, and I'd enjoy this opportunity to spend more time with my parent.

Summary:

Overall, how long do you estimate you could maintain your PRESENT lifestyle—purchases, activities, house, car, and all other aspects of your material life—if you suddenly lost all or a significant part of your current income (circle one)?

Two weeks

One month

Two months

Three months

Six months to a year

A year or longer

"But is that bad?" you may be asking. You tell me. How secure do you feel knowing that you are just that far away from being homeless or "deprived" of your luxuries? How comfortable are YOU living from paycheck to paycheck?

Quickly write down five words or phrases that reflect how you FEEL about your financial situation right now:

1. _____

2. _____

3. _____

4. _____

5. _____

Exercise #10

The Financial Mirror

Check all the items below that, deep down inside, you KNOW apply to your finances:

**Yes,
That's Me**

❑   1. Huge house payments (even if the house isn't huge)

❑   2. Fat car payments

❑   3. Sloppy large student loans

❑   4. Bloated credit cards

❑   5. Skinny savings account

❑   6. No budget

❑   7. Anorexic retirement account

❑   8. Past due bills

❑   9. Periodically overdrawn checking account

❑   10. Frequent faking before others that I have more money than I really have

❑   11. Sad face because my money runs out before the month runs out

❑   12. Out-of-control panic about my financial future if things don't change

If you have checked even ONE of these items, trade in your DENIAL for DETERMI-NATION to do something about your financial fitness!

Key Concept #2

If You Don't Do Anything . . . Things Will Get Worse!

Many people think that if they don't do ANYTHING about their current money situation, magically and mystically and miraculously, things will get better. They are wrong. Things will get WORSE.

The old story goes that if you drop a frog into boiling water, he will sense the pain and immediately jump out. But if you put a frog in room-temperature water, he will happily swim around in it. You can gradually turn the water up to the boiling point, and the frog won't sense the change or react to it . . . and in the end, he will boil to death.

That's where millions of Americans are when it comes to their financial state. They are unfit financially but believe deep down inside that fitness WILL occur without any effort on their part. They aren't aware that the "temperature" of their debt is just getting warmer and warmer.

What About You?

Are you truly better off financially today than you were last year, or last decade? I challenge you to do the next exercise!

Exercise #11

More or Less?

Section One

In each statement below, circle the word or phrase that applies to you.

I made **MORE / LESS** money this year than last year.

I made **MORE / LESS** money this year than five years ago.

I made **MORE / LESS** money this year than ten years ago.

I made **MORE / LESS** money this year than fifteen years ago.

Section Two

Base your responses to the next set of questions on what you truly believe to be reasonable, given your current financial situation, job security, and the future of your current career. Don't factor in windfalls such as winning a lottery or landing a new "dream salary" job.

I expect to make **MORE / LESS** money next year than this year.

I expect to make **SIGNIFICANTLY MORE / ABOUT THE SAME / LESS** money five years from now than I made five years ago.

I expect to make **SIGNIFICANTLY MORE / ABOUT THE SAME / LESS** money ten years from now than I expect to make next year.

Section Three

Base your answers on the total DOLLAR amount of all debt—including car payments, credit cards, and any other loan or indebtedness that you are "paying off" on a regular basis that is NOT your house payment or a payment on an investment piece of property.

I have **MORE / LESS** total debt this year than I had last year.

I have **MORE / LESS** total debt this year than five years ago.

I have **MORE / LESS** total debt this year than ten years ago.

I have **MORE / LESS** total debt this year than fifteen years ago.

Section Four

Take a look again at your answers to the above three sections and answer honestly:

I expect to have **MORE / LESS** income and **MORE / LESS** debt this next year than this year.

　　Given the trend, if I don't make any adjustments . . .

I expect to have **MORE / LESS** income and **MORE / LESS** debt five years from now than I had this past year.

Do you like the trend you see?

Most people, if they are really honest with themselves, see that their DEBT has risen even as their income has risen. They aren't really getting "ahead"— the numbers associated with income and debt BOTH are getting higher as the years pass.

Most people, if they are really honest in their projections, must admit that they MAY have greater income in the coming years, but they are also likely to have GREATER debt.

And, if you are nearing retirement, the likelihood is that you will have LESS income and either a sustaining or only slightly lower debt level in the next few years.

I don't know about you, but those trends make me nervous. They do not speak of a GOOD future, but rather a future that is increasingly bleak.

Key Concept #3
Denial Is Not the Same as Being Uninformed

There are some people who are uninformed about their finances. They have never really stopped to evaluate their financial situation. They don't know how to make a budget and, therefore, have never made one or attempted to live by one. They simply "don't know" about assets and liabilities.

In some cases, this ignorance comes about because one spouse allows another spouse—or a parent allows a child, or a grown child allows a parent—to make all the financial decisions and conduct all the financial transactions. These people are willfully ignorant. They don't think they need to know about money and, therefore, they don't learn about their own finances.

Living in denial is a very different case. Denial is *knowing* the numbers related to your financial condition but choosing to ignore them and to live as if you didn't know them.

It's not good to be either financially uninformed or financially in denial. I strongly encourage you to become both smart and wise—smart in "knowing" where you stand financially, and wise in "facing" the fact that you may be standing in financial quicksand.

What About You?

Are you financially smart—informed about where your money is, how much you actually have, and what you actually need on a monthly or an annual basis?

Are you financially wise—realistic, facing the facts, living in the reality that the financial decisions of today will greatly impact your financial well-being tomorrow?

Case Study: Jim

Jim graduated from college at the age of twenty-two and felt ready to take on the world. He got a good entry-level job working for a respectable business in his community—at a starting salary of $28,000 a year—and felt that he was on his way.

He was shocked when the bills started pouring in. While in college, Jim had lived in the dorm and eaten most of his meals in the college cafeteria—both of which had been paid for by his parents and school loans. He had worked part-time, which had provided money for gasoline for his truck, a couple of pizzas every week, and an occasional date. His part-time income also allowed him to pay "the minimum" on several credit cards.

Out of college, Jim soon discovered that he had not only apartment rent and grocery bills to pay, but also utility bills, cable TV and phone bills, and within a few months, school loans to repay. To compound his problem, he had charged several hundred dollars on both existing and newly issued credit cards to purchase items he felt he needed to start out life in an apartment of his own.

After six months of being in an apartment alone, Jim was having serious difficulty making ends meet. He felt angry that he no longer seemed to be as "well off" as he had been in the dorm—there wasn't even enough money for the pizzas and dates he had once enjoyed!

Jim read a few magazine articles and got a few opinions from older friends and came to the conclusion that he would take out a "consolidation loan" to cover his credit-card bills and school loans. He reasoned, "I have a $20,000 truck . . . surely I can get a loan for $10,000."

Wrong. Jim's grandfather had given him the truck when he was a sophomore in college, and by the time he sought a loan against it, the truck had depreciated to the point where it was valued at less than $10,000. Not only that, he quickly learned that no bank in his city would issue a loan for that amount against a depreciating "asset" such as a vehicle. Neither would a bank give him a loan for $10,000 based on his annual income in a job he had held for less than a year.

Reality hit hard. Jim eventually decided that he would take in a roommate to help "pay the bills." He didn't *want* to share his one-bedroom apartment with anybody, but he *had* to. He cut up his credit cards and went to a cash-only payment policy. He decided that he'd just have to make due with the furnishings and cookware and ten-year-old stereo system that he presently had—all of which were adequate, just not very "in" when it came to style or the latest technology. He gave up cable TV and several magazine subscriptions. And he learned to cook!

"Cooking was a good thing to learn," Jim later said, "but I did get tired of warmed-up cans of beans after a while. When I graduated from college, I had no idea how expensive it is to eat out *every* meal. Frankly,

I didn't know what a steak cost, much less a head of lettuce or a box of spaghetti."

Jim requested and was granted a one-year deferrment on his school loans, which accelerated his ability to pay off his credit cards. The credit-card debt was erased within twenty-one months. He then began to accelerate his repayment of the school loans, which should be paid off in three more years.

"I've been dreaming about a new truck," Jim admitted, "but a few weeks ago I decided that I didn't really need a new truck—I just *wanted* one. I'm thinking now that I might see about purchasing a small house so I really will have an asset to my name. The truck can come later—and I'll probably get one that's a couple of years old so I won't have the big depreciation hit."

Jim is starting to get smart about money.

Exercise #12

Smart About Money

The place to start in becoming financially smart is to make a very simple list of all your money assets and liabilities—in other words, the money you have and the money you owe.

Take into consideration these two possibilities—which are in many people's lives very real *probabilities:*

1. Are you still or will you be paying on student loans in the years ahead? How much more do you anticipate having to pay?

2. Are you facing any major expenses that MUST be made in the coming months or year, such as an operation you know you need to have or relocation to a new city where you have taken a job?

Make note of this total amount on the next page:

Total of major expenditures I'm anticipating in the next six to twelve months for which I presently do not anticipate any reimbursement from an outside source:

$ _____

Add this figure to the total debt figure noted at the bottom of the "Consumer Equity Sheet" at the end of this chapter. Then compare your assets (value) to your bills (debt).

TOTAL CASH   TOTAL CASH
ASSETS $ _____   V.   BILLS: $ _____

Again, note the gap between the two numbers. (Subtract the smaller number from the larger number.)

The AMOUNT: $ _____

Does the amount reflect an ASSET or a BILL (circle one)?

ASSET   BILL

That's the reality you can expect this time next year UNLESS you do something to change your cash bills or cash assets.

Before you dissolve into a puddle of despair, I have GOOD NEWS! The good news, of course, is that you CAN make changes in both sides of this column, if you are willing to do so. Being smart about money doesn't automatically mean you will be wise—it doesn't mean that you won't close this workbook and continue to live in denial. But being smart about money CAN give you the desire and the starting block from which to run a good race toward erasing the gap between bills and money assets—in fact, toward generating a better column of solid cash assets and NO cash bills.

We'll discuss in future chapters how to erase that gap, but for now, the purpose of SEEING these numbers is so that you are better informed about your money! It's one more glimpse into the mirror.

Don't count on "what-ifs" when it comes to estimating your assets. Count only on the cash-register *cha-ching* at the time of the sale!

(*NOTE:* To determine your entire "equity," complete the CONSUMER EQUITY SHEET at the end of this chapter.)

Exercise #13

"Before Picture" Snapshot

Early in this chapter I asked you to ESTIMATE what you believe to be the state of your current finances. After completing the exercises in this chapter, what is your CURRENT appraisal?

Very Fit   Moderately Fit   Somewhat Fit   Not Very Fit   NOT FIT!

Consider this the "before" snapshot of your financial fitness level. It isn't your goal. It isn't who you COULD be with some work; it's where you are starting out. If you are willing to "get real" with yourself, you can "get real" with your money.

Exercise #14

Your Self-Analysis

In each of the ten sentences that follow, circle the capitalized word or phrase that you believe to be most accurate:

1. Most people are **BETTER OFF / WORSE OFF** financially than they think they are.

2. **SEVENTY PERCENT / THIRTY PERCENT** of all Americans live from paycheck to paycheck.

3. It is better to live in **DENIAL / DETERMINATION** when it comes to money.

4. If a person does nothing about his or her financial situation, things will get **BETTER / WORSE.**

5. The trend in the lives of most Americans is toward **GREATER DEBT / LESS DEBT** in the next five years.

6. The trend described above is **TRUE / NOT TRUE** for my life, even though I hope and expect to be earning more money.

7. The gap between the money I have and the money I owe tells me that I have **MORE CASH ASSETS / MORE CASH BILLS.**

8. **I LIKE / DON'T LIKE** my overall financial situation.

9. I am **UNINFORMED / IN DENIAL** about money . . . but I don't want to be.

10. I am **DETERMINED TO CHANGE / UNWILLING TO CHANGE** my financial situation.

There really are no "right" or "wrong" answers when it comes to your personal feelings or opinions, but here's MY opinion about your feelings:

Responses to Statements 1–5: If you answered these statements with the following answers, you are well on your way to becoming more informed about money: worse off; seventy percent; determination; worse; greater debt.

Responses to Statements 6–10: How you answered these statements could very well be an indication about whether you are in denial about your financial situation. Take another look at your answers and you make the call.

• Do you need to become more financially fit? **YES / NO**

• Are you willing to make the changes necessary to become more financially fit? **YES / NO**

CONSUMER EQUITY SHEET

ITEM / DESCRIBE	VALUE	-	DEBT	=	EQUITY
Real Estate _____	$90,000		$70,000		$20,000
Real Estate _____					
Car _____					
Car _____	$7,000		$10,000		- $3,000
Cash on Hand					
Checking Account					
Checking Account					
Savings Account	$1,000		0		$1,000
Savings Account					
Money Market Account					
Mutual Funds					
Retirement Plan	$7,000		0		$7,000
Stocks or Bonds					
Cash Value (Insurance)					
Household Items					
Jewelry					
Antiques					
Boat					
Unsecured Debt (Neg.)	0		$7,000		- $7,000
Credit Card Debt (Neg.)					
Other _____					
Other _____					
Other _____					
TOTAL	$105,000		$87,000		$18,000

CONSUMER EQUITY SHEET

ITEM / DESCRIBE	VALUE	-	DEBT	=	EQUITY
Real Estate _____	_____		_____		_____
Real Estate _____	_____		_____		_____
Car _____	_____		_____		_____
Car _____	_____		_____		_____
Cash on Hand	_____		_____		_____
Checking Account	_____		_____		_____
Checking Account	_____		_____		_____
Savings Account	_____		_____		_____
Savings Account	_____		_____		_____
Money Market Account	_____		_____		_____
Mutual Funds	_____		_____		_____
Retirement Plan	_____		_____		_____
Stocks or Bonds	_____		_____		_____
Cash Value (Insurance)	_____		_____		_____
Household Items	_____		_____		_____
Jewelry	_____		_____		_____
Antiques	_____		_____		_____
Boat	_____		_____		_____
Unsecured Debt (Neg.)	_____		_____		_____
Credit Card Debt (Neg.)	_____		_____		_____
Other _____	_____		_____		_____
Other _____	_____		_____		_____
Other _____	_____		_____		_____
TOTAL	_____		_____		_____

3

Debt Is (Not) a Tool:
DEBT MYTHS

Key Concept #1

You Must STOP Doing Some BAD Things Before You Can Do GOOD Things

For centuries the medical world has lived by the "first" rule of medicine, which is "DO NO HARM." Before a physician can ever do "good" for a patient, he needs to make sure that he is doing no harm.

Another basic phrase in medical practice is "First, stop the bleeding." Actually, in recent times, that's also a phrase a great many stockbrokers have used. Before anything constructive can be done to help a badly wounded person, any hemorrhaging that exists must be brought under control.

In the nutrition world, there's another simple rule: "Stop eating the bad stuff"—a vitally important part of becoming healthier as one begins to eat the "right" foods.

What does all this have to do with a Total Money Makeover? It is just as important for you to stop doing the "wrong" things with your money as it is for you to start doing the "right" things with your money.

The same goes for your beliefs and attitudes about money. Most people I meet grew up believing certain myths about debt and money—these myths are not only ineffective and unproductive, but they are very damaging to a person's finances. Still, as a nation, we continue to believe these myths and pass them on.

Stop the hemorrhaging . . . stop the myth believing . . . stop the bad money habits!

It's easier said than done. Why?

Because debt is part of our "I want it NOW" mind-set as a culture. Human nature screams out with a loud inner voice, "I've GOT to have this"—and we proceed to GET the item regardless of how much debt we take on with its acquisition.

So many lies are told in our world today about debt that the lies have taken on a ring of truth. If you tell a lie often enough, loud enough, and long enough, the lie begins to be accepted as a fact. That certainly seems to be what has happened when it comes to the lies about debt that are fed to us every day of every month of every year. The logic is twisted . . . the rationalization is intense and sometimes blatantly obvious . . . but, nonetheless, we buy the lie hook, line, and sinker and, in the end, we have become a nation of debtors.

Before we can begin to act on the TRUTH about how wealth is built, we need to confront the lies we've been taught, and, more important, we need to stop believing the lies.

What About You?

Have you bought into any lies about debt? Let's find out . . .

Exercise #15

What's Your View on Debt?

Respond to the statements that follow by checking either **TRUE** or **FALSE**.

TRUE FALSE

❑   ❑   1. I don't know anybody who doesn't have a car payment on their current automobile, or who didn't buy their current automobile using a payment plan of some type (including a leasing plan).

❑   ❑   2. I don't know anybody who graduated from a four-year college without taking out at least one student loan.

❑   ❑   3. I don't know anybody who has NO credit cards.

❑   ❑   4. I don't know anybody under the age of fifty who has a completely paid-for house.

❑   ❑   5. I don't know anybody who has paid cash (by writing a check, using a debit card) for every part of a two-week family vacation to a major resort.

The fact is, most people in our nation today believe that debt is NORMAL, and in most cases, NECESSARY. They can't imagine living a cash-and-carry life or a life in which all things they own are purchased outright with cash at the time of purchase—in other words, with no payment plan or use of credit cards.

Key Concept #2
Debt Is NOT a Good Tool for Creating Prosperity

One of the main myths we've been taught about debt is that debt is a necessary "tool" for creating prosperity.

The TRUTH is that debt adds considerable risk to life, and it does NOT generate prosperity.

Years ago when I began a career in real estate, I was told as part of my training program that debt was a tool—the exact phrase was that "debt is like a fulcrum and lever." My instructors taught me that it was GOOD to use OPM—other people's money—as a way of building personal wealth.

I'm a little ashamed to admit it now, but I sold rental property to a lot of investors on that very myth. I convinced investors that their borrowing of money to purchase rental property was a good thing. The line was this: Rental property had the potential for yielding greater and greater income to the property owner, and since property values were sure to rise, the purchase of rental property would soon give the owner equity that the owner could borrow against to purchase still more rental property. Fine in theory, but also potentially disastrous in real life.

What happens if one of the rental properties needs major repairs or fails to stay rented? What happens if property values go DOWN, not up? The house of cards can come tumbling down in a big hurry.

Those who believe this myth about debt being a "tool" may not have been burned by it, but I have been. I went through bankruptcy and lost virtually everything but my wife and my health as a result of believing that debt is a "tool" for generating prosperity.

What those who perpetuate this lie never tell you is this: All money loaned to you CAN be required from you by the lender of the money, generally on the lender's terms and timetable. In other words, they never tell you about the RISK associated with debt. And believe me, all debt has a shadow of risk associated with it.

They also never tell you that the genuinely wealthy people among us rarely use debt as a tool. The Forbes 400, which is a list of the four hundred wealthiest people in America according to *Forbes* magazine, once surveyed their list, and 75 percent said that the BEST way to build wealth is to become and stay debt-free. Some of America's most prosperous companies, including Walgreens, Microsoft, and Harley–Davidson, are all run debt-free.

What About You?

Let me ask you three questions:

First, are you better off or worse off financially because you have and use credit cards? (The vast majority of people have credit-card balances that are NOT paid off every month. That balance is charged an interest fee—which is a payment the card holder makes but receives nothing in return to show for the money paid out.)

Second, are you better off or worse off financially because you buy an automobile with a five- or six-year loan? (You can't be better off financially because such a payment plan just about doubles the cost of the car once you factor in the total amount of interest you pay on the loan.)

Third, is your credit rating really any better because you took out that loan for college tuition? (It certainly isn't better if you missed a payment or two. And if you go to get still MORE debt in the form of a house loan, a large outstanding student loan CAN be considered a detriment, not an asset.)

Exercise #16

Did You Know?

See how well you do in completing the following sentences using the Word Pool below:

1. In 1910, the Sears catalog stated, "Buying on _____ is folly." Nearly a hundred years later, Sears now makes more money on the interest paid on its credit-card accounts than it does on the sale of merchandise.

2. The founder of JC Penney department stores was a man nicknamed James "_____" Penney because he personally detested the use of debt or making time payments. Today, Penney's makes millions each year on their customers who use plastic.

3. Henry Ford thought debt was a _____ man's method of purchasing items. As a result of Ford's belief, the Ford Motor Company did not offer financing plans until ten years after General Motors offered them. Today, however, Ford Motor Credit is one of the most profitable divisions of Ford Motor's operations.

4. Proverbs 22:7 says, "The rich rules over the _____, and the borrower is _____ to the lender."

5. Beverly Sills had it right when she said, "There is no _____ to any place worth going."

6. If you want to know how to get and stay skinny, talk to skinny people. If you want to know how wealthy people get and stay wealthy, talk to _____ people.

Word Pool

servant • lazy • cash • shortcut • wealthy • credit • poor

Answers:

1. credit

2. cash

3. lazy

4. poor; servant

5. shortcut

6. wealthy

Go back and read aloud each of these statements with the correct words filling the blanks!

Key Concept #3
One of the Best Ways to Lose a Friend
Is to Loan Money to That Friend

Another major lie we have been taught about debt is that we are "helping" a friend or relative when we loan that person money. The truth is, you are likely to seriously strain or even destroy your relationship with a friend or relative to whom you loan money.

What About You?

Do you know how to say no to a friend or relative?

Case Study: Joan

Joan called my radio program one afternoon. Very distraught, she felt she had ruined her relationship with one of her best friends.

Onc of Joan's colleagues at work was a single mother who was broke and needed $50 to tide her over to payday. Joan knew this woman well—in fact, she had lunch with her every day and had been her confidante and sounding board. Joan quickly and sympathetically loaned her friend the $50 she said she needed.

Payday came . . . and payday went. Joan's friend made no mention of the money she had borrowed. In fact, she began to go out of her way to avoid seeing Joan. In a very subtle but very real way, guilt and shame had entered Joan's relationship with this woman, along with a certain amount of disappointment, disillusionment, and even a touch of anger on Joan's part.

All for the want of $50.

"What can I do?" Joan asked.

I asked Joan if her friendship with this woman was worth $50. She gushed that she believed their friendship was worth many times that. "Then call your friend or e-mail her a note and tell her that the debt is forgiven. The money you gave her was a GIFT."

Joan was willing to do this, but she also asked, "Is this really helping my friend? What if she asks me for money again, or what if she continues this habit with other people? Am I doing her a favor in the long run by ignoring her failure to repay this borrowed money?"

I suggested, "Put two stipulations on your canceling of the debt. Ask her to agree with you that she will help someone in need someday with an outright gift of $50 . . . and ask her to agree with you that she will never loan any money to her friends." I told Joan that if her friend would agree to these two stipulations, it was highly unlikely she would ever ask Joan for money again.

If you GIVE money to a friend, you get the joy of giving and your friend has the pleasure of RECEIVING. If you LOAN money to a friend, however, your friend is suddenly no longer an equal in the friendship—rather your friend is "under" you in a way that's difficult to explain psychologically but true nonetheless. You will have changed the power balance in the relationship to suddenly being "on top," with your borrowing friend "below." Resentment can build in both persons, as well as a great deal of anxiety, frustration, and even anger.

Avoid the hassle and keep your friendships as FRIENDSHIPS. Don't loan money to friends or relatives!

Exercise #17

You as Lender . . . or Borrower

I invite you to put yourself in the position of LENDER or BORROWER in each of the situations described below. Using fewer than ten words, describe how you would feel if this happened to YOU.

Situation #1

LENDER: As a parent of a twenty-five-year-old son, who has recently married a twenty-five-year-old wife, you have loaned the couple $5,000 to use as a down payment for their first home. Six months after the couple are in the new home, you get word from your son that he and his wife are planning a vacation to Hawaii. Not a dime has yet been paid back to you of the money you loaned to them. How do you feel?

BORROWER: You are twenty-five years old, and your mother-in-law six months ago loaned you and your husband $5,000 to use as a down payment on your first home. You recently were in the room when your husband told his mother you are going on a trip to Hawaii in a few weeks. You caught a disapproving look from her, and you know it has to do with your spending money on a trip when you haven't started paying her back yet on the down-payment loan. How do you feel?

Situation #2

LENDER: You are a grandfather who loves your twenty-year-old grandson a great deal. You loan Junior $25,000 for a new four-wheel-drive truck he "needs" to get to and from work. You loan him the money at 6 percent interest, which is a better deal than he can get at a bank. You use a CD you have at the bank to make the purchase. Junior loves the truck. Junior loves you. You love Junior and are happy to help. Then Junior loses his job and can't pay back the loan. Months go by with no repayment of the money. You and Junior argue about the debt, and Junior up and sells the truck for $19,000 and gives you the money as if that's the total he owes you. He makes it very clear that he is angry with you for expecting the money to be repaid. You suspect that you are never going to see the other $6,000 . . . and may not see Junior again either. How do you feel?

BORROWER: You are twenty years old and are driving an old jalopy that sometimes gets you to work on time, and sometimes breaks down so you can't get to work at all.

You know Gramps has some money, so you ask him if he'd be willing to loan you money for a vehicle. Actually, you've already seen a four-wheel-drive truck that suits you just perfectly! Gramps agrees to loan you the money, and within a matter of days the truck is yours. Then, for reasons that are really no fault of yours, you are let go from your job. The job market is tight, and you miss several payments. Gramps is upset and starts asking you about the money. You feel pressured and finally decide you don't need this hassle. You sell the truck, but the best you can get for it is $19,000. You give that to Gramps, who still seems to expect MORE. How do you feel?

Key Concept #4
Don't Get Involved in "Rip-Off" Possibilities

There are a number of situations that I describe as "rip-offs just waiting to happen." People fall into these traps every day, and usually seem surprised when what seemed like an "okay deal" jumps up to bite them. Generally speaking, lower-income people fall for these rip-off deals, which only ensures that they will remain at the bottom of the socioeconomic ladder.

If a deal has "quick" associated with it, beware. If the deal involves the idea of "get it now, pay later," run.

What About You?

Do you know a potential rip-off when you see one? Let's see . . .

Exercise #18

Rip-Off Quiz

Check TRUE or FALSE for each of the statements on the next page:

TRUE FALSE

☐ ☐ 1. I believe in helping people when I can, and I am flattered at the opportunity to help a friend or relative by co-signing a loan.

☐ ☐ 2. A "cash advance" or "payday loan" is a good way to handle an emergency until payday.

☐ ☐ 3. If you can't afford an item outright, "rent-to-own" is a good way to purchase items such as furniture and appliances.

☐ ☐ 4. If you need transportation right away and don't have much money, a "Tote the Note" car is better than no car at all.

☐ ☐ 5. One of the best ways to make a major purchase is "ninety days same as cash."

☐ ☐ 6. Debt consolidation is usually a smart idea if you have lots of debts.

☐ ☐ 7. It's a smart deal to get a second mortgage and finance a house for more than it's worth if it allows you to restructure your debt.

If you marked TRUE for any of the above answers, you definitely need to read the next couple of pages. If you don't know WHY each of the above statements is false, you also need the information below.

Explanation of the Answers:

1. *Co-Signing Statement:* I believe in helping people when I can, and I am flattered at the opportunity to help a friend or relative by co-signing a loan. FALSE!

Why this is FALSE: Some people believe that if you "co-sign" a loan for a friend or relative, you aren't really lending money to that friend . . . you are just giving your signature.

Not so. From the perspective of the person making the loan, with your signature you have just become the borrower!

There's a reason the bank or other lending institution is requiring a cosigner on the loan. The reason is, the bank doesn't truly believe the applicant will be able to pay the full amount of the loan. In the end, they believe YOU can . . . and will.

Now if the lending institution—which has lots of experience in loaning money—doesn't fully trust the person to repay the loan, why should you?

At least a couple of times a week I get a caller to *The Dave Ramsey Show* who tells me the final chapter of a co-signing experience. I can sum up the results in five words: "broken heart and broken dreams."

Parents are disillusioned that their child defaults on a loan. They thought they "raised" their child better than that.

A person is frustrated that a mortgage lender won't grant a loan because of a "co-signed" note he made five years before.

A man is angry and hurt that the girlfriend for whom he had co-signed a note has skipped town and can't be found.

The stories go on and on.

2. *Cash-Advance and Payday-Loan Statement:* A "cash advance" or "payday loan" is a good way to handle an emergency until payday. FALSE!

Why this is FALSE: The payday loan is one of the fastest-growing trash lenders. The procedure: You write a hot check for $225 dated for one week from now—payday. The lender gives you $200 cash on the spot. In the first place, writing a bad check at any time or under any circumstance is illegal. Apart from that, the lender in this case is charging what amounts to 650 percent interest annually! (That's what $25 for one week on $200 amounts to.)

3. *Rent-to-Own Statement:* If you can't afford an item outright, "rent to own" is a good way to purchase items such as furniture and appliances. FALSE!

Why this is FALSE: The Federal Trade Commission continues to investigate this industry because the effective interest rates in most of these transactions amount to 1,800 percent on average! For example, the average washer and dryer generally run $20 a week for ninety weeks. That's a whopping $1,800 for a washer and dryer! A new washer and dryer, at full retail price, can be purchased for $500 and a slightly used set of these appliances for about $200. If a person saved just $20 a week for ten weeks, he could have purchased a scratch-or-dent, off-the-floor model. Surely a person can go to a Laundromat for ten weeks!

4. *The Tote-the-Note Statement:* If you need transportation right away and don't have much money, a "Tote the Note" car is better than no car at all. FALSE!

Why this is FALSE: Most of these schemes involve older, cheaper cars. The dealer purchases the car and sells it for a down payment that is equal to what he paid for the car. That way the payments—usually at 18 percent to 38 percent interest paid weekly—all amount to profit for the lender. Many of these cars are repeatedly repossessed because people can't pay the high interest rates, which leaves the "buyer" once again out of transportation and out some cash. If the car can be sold yet again, the lender continues to rake in the profits. Don't be duped. Take public transportation or pay for the gasoline of a friend who will provide transportation for you until you can scrape together a few hundred dollars to buy a reliable car outright—no payments, no interest.

5. *Ninety-Days-Same-as-Cash Statement:* One of the best ways to make a major purchase is "ninety days same as cash." FALSE!

Why this is FALSE: This is one of the silliest marketing ploys America has fallen for. First, ninety days is NOT the same as cash. If you flash several hundred-dollar bills in front of a manager who has a sales quota, you probably can get a discount on just about any major item (such as furniture, electronics, or appliances). If cash can get you a discount, then cash is the better deal!

Second, MOST people don't pay off the debt in the allotted time—in fact, 88 percent of these contracts convert to debt, and the debt is usually charged at a very high interest rate of from 24 percent to 38 percent, which is *charged back to the date of purchase!*

Third, if you paid $1,000 for an item over a ninety-day period, think about the advantage of saving up, paying cash for the item, and then investing that same $1,000 for ninety days. Even at only 3 percent annual interest, you'd make about $7.50 in ninety days. It's not much, but it's a PLUS instead of a MINUS.

Fourth and finally, many of these contracts have little clauses related to "insurance" that some consumers inadvertently sign—and in at least one case I know, the box was initialed by a salesperson, and the person who was "ripped off" found it cheaper to pay the charge of $174 rather than hire an attorney and handwriting expert to prove his point. If you aren't willing to sit down and read the entire "ninety days same as cash" agreement, don't sign it.

6. *Debt-Consolidation Statement:* Debt consolidation is usually a smart idea if you have lots of debts. FALSE!

Why this is FALSE: You haven't erased any debt with a debt-consolidation loan . . . you've just moved it around a little. In most cases, you've dug the hole deeper. Plus, you still have the spending habits that caused the debt in the first place. The internal statistics of those in the business of making consolidation loans show that in 78 percent of the cases, the debt grows back. People are still in a get-it-now and pay-for-it-later mind-set, and they simply take on MORE debt.

Many people buy into this idea because they believe a lower monthly payment on the consolidation loan will help them financially. What they fail to realize is that they may be paying less per month, but they are paying for a lot *longer* time period. If you stay in debt longer, you pay the lender more! That's why people seek to make these loans.

7. *Second-Mortgage-for-More-Than-House-Value Statement:* It's a smart deal to get a second mortgage and refinance a house for more than it's worth, if it allows you to restructure your debt. FALSE!

Why this is FALSE: You're still in the house, and if you ever need to sell it, you are in serious trouble. Some people who have lost their homes find they are still paying on a second mortgage loan long after they no longer have the house to live in.

Why do people seek to take out second mortgages? Usually because they want to erase credit-card debt, medical bills, or other bills. The better approach is to take on those bills one at a time and leave all the equity you can in your house.

Key Concept #5
Get Smart About Buying an Automobile

The vast majority of people in our nation have bought into the lie that car payments are a way of life and a person will always have one.

As far as I'm concerned, the car payment is one of the top three dumb things people do to destroy their chances of building wealth. For most people who are making monthly car payments, this is their next highest monthly payment after a home mortgage or in some cases, rent. The average car payment today is $378 over fifty-five months. Generally speaking, once a person gets a car paid in full, he or she trades in that car and takes out another loan for a new car. That means the $378-a-month payment lasts pretty much all a person's life— usually from about age twenty-five to age sixty-five (at which point people finally seem to realize they don't need a new car every four to six years).

If a person INVESTED $378 a month from age twenty-five to sixty-five at 12 percent (the seventy-year stock-market average), the person would have $4,447,094.01. That's a lot of car!

If a person put $378 a month into a cookie jar or a simple 1 to 2 percent-interest-bearing checking account, he'd have close to $4,000 at the end of ten months. That's enough to buy a vehicle outright—no payment!

Now, I'm not suggesting that you drive a $4,000 car your entire life, but that is a way to get a car without debt. If you save the $378 a month for the next year, you can trade up to an $8,000 car a year later . . . Keep saving, and in a couple of years you can have a $12,000 or $16,000 car.

What about leasing? People these days seem to think that leasing an automobile is what sophisticated people do. The pitch is that a person should lease things that go down in value and that have tax advantages.

The truth is that consumer advocates, financial experts, magazines such as *Consumer Reports* and *Smart Money,* and a good calculator all will tell you that leasing a car is the most expensive way to operate a vehicle. You in essence are "renting to own." (Read the previous section of this workbook!)

The Federal Trade Commission requires a truth-in-lending statement when a person purchases a car or gets a mortgage, but this is NOT required for a lease. The result is that people have no idea what interest rate they are paying on a lease. The average is somewhere around 14 percent!

The problem is that we don't ask, "How much?" anymore. We ask, "How much down and how much a month?"

What About You?

Are you making car payments today? Are you leasing a vehicle? Or are you at least CONSIDERING buying a car and making payments or leasing a vehicle? Let me walk you through a simple exercise.

Exercise #19

How Much for this Doggy in the Car Showroom Window?

Deal #1

From the three dollar amounts provided below, choose the amount that you believe belongs in each of the blanks in the sentences below. These figures are from the National Auto Dealers Association (NADA) as reported in *Smart Money* magazine.

$1,300 • $82 • $775

1. The average new car purchase for CASH makes a dealer an _____ profit.

2. The average car purchased using a "financing contract"—payments made over time—yields the dealer _____ .

3. The average lease deal yields the dealer _____ .

Answers:

  1. $82

  2. $775

  3. $1,300

Go back and read aloud each of these statements with the correct figures filling the blanks! Any questions about why the dealer was pushing you to "lease"?

Deal #2

A dealer offers you a lease on a $22,000 NEW car for $416 a month for four years. He advises you that if you use the vehicle for business only, you can deduct that amount—about $5,000 for a year—from your taxes as a business expense. There are two major flaws in this—can you identify them?

Answer:

1. Very few vehicles are used EXCLUSIVELY for business—most times a leased car will not survive an IRS audit on just this point. If you DID save the $5,000 on your taxes . . . well, you've still given the car leasing company the $5,000, so you are out $5,000. Tax on $5,000 would be about $1,500. You are out a net $3,500, even if you do qualify for the deduction!

2. There's a big clue related to these deals—they are for NEW cars. Why? Because the dealer wants you to buy a NEW car. The higher the purchase price, the more he makes.

The fact is, a new car loses 60 percent of its value in the first four years. If you buy a $28,000 car at 0 percent, you will lose $17,000 of that in the next forty-eight months.

On the other hand, if you buy a four-year-old USED car with CASH for $17,000 . . . you aren't going to lose much at all over the forty-eight months after your purchase.

"But what about the warranty?" you may say. Some people opt for a new car because they want a warranty for their vehicle. If a warranty costs you $17,000 in value over a four-year period, that's an expensive warranty! You could have your car engine completely rebuilt several times for that amount.

Case Study: The Amazing Free Car

Here's what Americans usually buy: An $18,000 car, purchased over seven years at 10 percent interest, with monthly payments of $300. The value of the car after seven years is $800.

Here's what we could do instead: Buy a $6,000 used car, purchased over seven years at 10 percent interest, with monthly payments of $100. The value of the car after seven years is $400.

Invest the $200 difference each month at 10 percent for the seven years of the car loan. That $200 a month will grow over those seven years into $24,190.

When the seven years are up . . .

Both cars are junk.

If you opted for the new, innovative plan that started with a $6,000 car, by now you have $24,190. Take $16,000 of that and buy the best one-year-old used car you can find for $16,000. This leaves $8,190 in the investments account to continue to grow at 10 percent. Drive this car for seven years with NO CAR PAYMENTS.

Nevertheless, pretend you have a car payment. Add $300 a month from year seven to year fourteen to the $8,190 you have in the investments account. At the end of year fourteen, you will have $52,245 in the investments account! Take $25,000 out of that investments account to buy the best one-year-old car you can find for $25,000. Leave the rest in the investments account to grow for another seven years. You'll have NO CAR PAYMENTS THE REST OF YOUR LIFE and have a relatively new car every seven years!

Exercise #20

Drive Like a Millionaire

Complete the blanks below to the best of your guess-ability!

1. The average millionaire purchases a _____ car.
   a. one-year-old
   b. new
   c. two-year-old
   d. three-year-old

2. The average millionaire has a _____ monthly car payment.

   a. $500

   b. $650

   c. $350

   d. $0

3. If you are driving a used, fully-paid-for car for business purposes, you can still get a tax benefit by:

   a. taking straight-line depreciation on an expensive car that has very few miles a year put on it

   b. taking a mileage deduction on an inexpensive car that you put high mileage on each year

   c. both a and b

   d. neither a nor b

Answers:

1. (c.) The average millionaire purchases a TWO-year-old car.

2. (d.) The average millionaire has $0 in car payment.

3. (c.) If you are driving a used, fully paid-for car for business purposes, you can still get a tax benefit by taking straight-line depreciation on an expensive car that has very few miles a year put on it, or by taking a mileage deduction on an inexpensive car that you put high mileage on each year.

Case Study: Dave

I went through bankruptcy when I was in my twenties, and I dropped from driving a Jaguar into driving a borrowed, 400,000-mile Cadillac that had a vinyl roof torn loose so it filled up with air like a parachute.

The predominant color on this car was Bondo. I drove "Bondo Buggy" for three months, which seemed like ten years to me. No fun!

But I quickly realized that if I was willing to be smart about buying cars and paying cash for them, I could one day drive a luxury car again.

If you insist on driving new cars with payments your entire life, you will literally blow a life's fortune on cars. But if you are willing to sacrifice for a while, you can have your life's fortune AND drive a quality car. I opt for the millionaire strategy.

Key Concept #6
Get Smart About Credit Cards

The lies related to credit cards are almost too numerous to list! Let's be sure about one main fact: When you use your credit card, you are taking out a LOAN.

If you pay off that loan in thirty days, with MOST credit or charge cards you don't pay interest. In some cases, however, you start paying interest from the day you use the card.

If you don't pay off the loan in thirty days, you can COUNT on interest, and it's high—MUCH higher than any other type of bank loan. We used to call credit cards "charge cards." Then somebody in a marketing department probably got smart and said, "Hey, people are going to figure out that when they use their 'charge card' we in the bank are actually charging them!" *Credit card* sounded a lot better—it sounded as if the person was doing something good. To get a "credit card," a person had to have good credit, right? That certainly isn't true today. Nevertheless, the myths prevail. The fact is, charge cards really do continue to charge you, at rates that can vary widely. I recently talked to one woman who had several charge cards that were charging her from 9 percent to 21 percent.

What About You?

Do you have credit cards in your wallet or purse? How many do you have? WHY do you have them?

Exercise #21

Credit-Card Crazy

Let's see what you know about credit cards! Indicate whether you think each statement is true or false.

TRUE FALSE

❑ ❑   1. You should get a credit card to build your credit.

❑ ❑   2. The debit card has more risk than a credit card.

❑ ❑   3. You need a credit card to rent a car, check in to a hotel, or make a purchase "on-line."

❑ ❑   4. Giving your teenager a credit card is a way to teach your child how to be responsible about money.

❑ ❑   5. If you pay your credit-card balance off every month, you get "free use" of their money.

❑ ❑   6. A credit card is a great way to chalk up "bonus" points or airline miles.

Answers:

  1. false   4. false

  2. false   5. false

  3. false   6. false

If you marked TRUE to any of these, read the next section carefully.

1. *You should get a credit card to build your credit.* FALSE!

Bankers, car dealers, and unknowledgeable mortgage lenders have told us for years to "build our credit." The basic underlying principle they believe is that you have to have debt to get MORE debt, because debt is how we buy stuff. The truth is, however, that cash buys stuff better than debt. The reason bankers, car dealers, and unknowledgeable, or unethical, mortgage lenders tell you to "build your credit" is because THEY want to earn the interest you are going to be paying them.

"But," you may say, "I need credit to buy a home."

No, you don't. We'll deal with this later, but, basically, you need to find a mortgage company that does actual underwriting. This means they are professional enough to process the details of your life instead of using only a Beacon score related to credit. You can qualify for a fifteen-year fixed-rate loan if

- You have paid your landlord early or on time for two years.
- You have been in the same career field for two years.
- You have a good down payment, which is more than "nothing down."
- You have no other credit, good or bad.
- You are not trying to take on too big a loan. A payment that is equal or less than 25 percent of your total take-home pay is considered conservative and will help you qualify.

2. *The debit card has more risk than a credit card.* FALSE!

Visa's regulations require member banks to grant the debit card the exact same protections in cases of theft or fraud. If you question this, read Visa's Zero Liability policy statement on Visa's own Web site. If someone steals your debit card number while you're shopping, on-line or off, you pay nothing for their fraudulent activity. Just as with a credit card, you need to continually monitor your monthly statement to identify any unauthorized transactions.

3. *You need a credit card to rent a car, check in to a hotel, or make a purchase "on-line."* FALSE!

Use a debit card instead. A debt card gives you the ability to do virtually anything a credit card will do. I carry one debit card on my personal account and another debit card on my business account. I do not have ANY credit cards. There's one thing you need if you are using a debit card: money in your bank account. There's one thing a debit card won't do—get you into debt!

When it comes to car rentals, a few companies will not take a debit card—these companies tend to be the higher-priced ones anyway. Most rental car places do take debit cards. Check in advance.

4. *Giving your teenager a credit card is a way to teach your child how to be responsible about money.* FALSE!

The exact opposite is true. Why would you want to teach your child how to handle DEBT? Teach your child, instead, how to pay for things on a cash-and-go basis and to save for the things he or she wants rather than take out loans to buy things.

5. *If you pay your credit-card balance off every month, you get "free use" of their money.* FALSE!

The fact is, 78 percent of credit-card holders do NOT pay off their credit cards every month.

Credit-card users spend 12 to 18 percent more when using credit instead of cash. It hurts to spend cash, so you spend less.

6. *A credit card is a great way to chalk up "bonus" points or airline miles.* FALSE!

Not really. You MIGHT acquire bonus points or airline miles, but this isn't a GREAT reason to use a credit card. *Consumer Reports* has noted that 75 percent of all airline miles are never redeemed. The same is true for many of the bonus-point plans. What do millionaires do? They don't get rich with free hats, brownie points, or air miles. Broke people use credit cards.

Exercise #22

A Little Credit-Card Quiz

See how much you *really* know about using credit cards:

1. According to the American Bankruptcy Institute study of bankruptcy filers, _____ percent of filers say credit-card debt caused the bankruptcy.
   a. 17
   b. 23
   c. 40
   d. 52
   e. 69

2. If you play long enough with snakes, you will eventually get
   a. tired of playing
   b. bitten
   c. scaly skin
   d. none of the above

3. More than _____ percent of graduating college seniors have credit-card debt before they even have a job.

   a. 15

   b. 31

   c. 47

   d. 70

   e. 80

4. According to the American Bankruptcy Institute, _____ percent of the people who filed for bankruptcy last year were college students.

   a. 7

   b. 13

   c. 19

   d. 30

   e. 40

Answers:

1. (e.) According to the American Bankruptcy Institute study of bankruptcy filers, 69 percent of filers say credit-card debt caused the bankruptcy. More than two-thirds of all bankruptcy filers surveyed by the American Bankruptcy institute said that credit-card debt was the main reason for their filing bankruptcy.

2. (b.) If you play long enough with snakes, you will eventually get BITTEN!

3. (e.) More than *80* percent of graduating college seniors have credit-card debt before they even have a job. How sad.

4. (c.) According to the American Bankruptcy Institute, *19* percent of the people who filed for bankruptcy last year were college students. That means nearly one in five bankruptcy filings a year are by young people who have already chalked up a major financial failure in their lives.

Key Concept #7

Beware of Debt "Management" Ideas

There are two main debt-management ideas that are widely publicized and, unfortunately, widely used.

Debt Consolidation

Whenever you come across the phrase "debt consolidation," think of it as debt CONsolidation. It's a con because it leads you to think you are doing something about your debt problem when you really aren't. You simply can't borrow your way out of debt. Internal statistics in firms that deal in debt consolidation estimate that as much as 78 percent of the time, people come to consolidate their "credit-card debt" but that after the consolidation, the debt amount grows rather than reduces. The reason is that people simply don't have a game plan for curbing their spending habits.

The most attractive advertised feature about debt consolidation plans is that the payment is lower. The reason for this, however, is usually that the payback period is extended. A lower rate for a longer time period means even MORE interest is being charged. It's a short-term, feel-good solution that really creates a longer-term problem!

Simple Q & A

Q: Ram Research Corporation states there are over _____ Discover, Citibank Visa, and American Express cards.

A: 147 million

Home-Mortgage Restructuring

Some programs are available that allow a person to borrow 125 percent of the home's value to restructure debt. What a dumb idea! You're stuck in the house. You have no collateral. If you lose your job, you're in big trouble.

Exercise #23

What Would Happen If . . .

1. What do you think would happen if every single American stopped using debt of any kind over the next fifty years?

   a. The economy would collapse.

   b. Everybody would prosper.

   c. Banks and other lenders would suffer, but the economy overall would prosper.

2. In a personal-debt-free economy, individual people would

   a. Save more, creating greater personal and national monetary stability.

   b. Spend more on goods and services (rather than on bank interest), which would boost the economy.

   c. Give more to charitable concerns.

   d. All of the above

3. If general giving to charitable causes increased,

   a. Many social problems could be resolved.

   b. Charitable concerns could be privatized.

   c. The government could get out of the welfare business.

   d. Taxes could be reduced, resulting in even greater personal wealth.

   e. All of the above.

Answers:

1. (c.) If every single American stopped using debt of any kind over the next fifty years, banks and other lenders would suffer, but the economy overall would prosper. The money shift would be into the hands of individual people rather than institutions.

2. (d.) In a personal-debt-free economy, individual people would save more (creating greater personal and national monetary stability), spend more on goods and services (rather than on bank interest, which would boost the economy), and give more to charitable concerns. How do we know that's true? Because that's what people who have worked themselves into a position of being independently wealthy generally do! All these behaviors are GOOD ones!

3. (e.) If general giving to charitable causes increased, many social problems could be resolved, charitable concerns could be privatized, and the government could get out of the welfare business. If the government didn't have to fund welfare, taxes could be greatly reduced, resulting in even greater personal wealth. In the words of Austin Powers, "Yeah, baby!"

BONUS Concept
Teach Your Children About Kid-Branding

Lenders are teaching kids earlier and earlier to rely on plastic to make purchases. Let me give you just two examples:

- A recent issue of Raisin Bran boxes featured a scene from *How the Grinch Stole Christmas*. What was touted as the official card of Whoville? VISA

- Mattel put out "Cool Shopping Barbie," who had her own MasterCard. When Barbie scanned her card, the cash register said, "Credit approved." Thank goodness there was such consumer backlash that Mattel pulled the product. A new toy brought out afterward, however, was "Barbie Cash Register," which comes with its own American Express card.

What's In Your Cupboard and Toy Box?

Check out your child's toy chest and your own cereal cupboard. Check out the packages of "kid food" items that you may be purchasing for your child. See how many "kid-branding" examples you can find!

4

The (Non) Secrets of the Rich:
MONEY MYTHS

Key Concept #1

There's a Price to Be Paid for Financial Fitness

People yearn to become healthy, wealthy, and wise with no effort and no risk. Life doesn't work that way.

There's no pill you can pop that will allow you to lose ten pounds overnight. There's no machine you can use two minutes once a week and become physically fit. And there's no easy fix for financial problems or an easy way to financial fitness.

Millions of people every year stay in jobs they hate because they think they are achieving financial security. They believe total safety is possible, and likely. They believe they have eliminated all risk. They are wrong.

Millions of dollars every year are spent on lotteries and other kinds of "gaming" in the hopes of getting rich quick. People are looking for the magic key to the treasure chest. They believe in easy wealth. They also are wrong.

What About You?

Are you living in denial today about your financial state or your financial future? Are you living in a FALSE sense of security? Let's find out . . .

Exercise #24

It's Smart to Know
What You Don't Know!

Indicate whether you believe each statement is true or false:

TRUE FALSE

❑ ❑ 1. The rich have "secrets." I just need to learn them.

❑ ❑ 2. I don't need to worry about retirement yet—I'll figure out something when I get to be that age.

❑ ❑ 3. I can get rich by working just a few hours a week, if I can just get trained and start selling the newest wonder product in a business I run out of my home.

❑ ❑ 4. I just need to learn how to buy and sell real estate with "no money down" to get rich.

❑ ❑ 5. I just need to find a way to get in on the tips related to hot stock deals.

❑ ❑ 6. There's real money to be made in becoming my own "day-trader" stockbroker.

Answers:

1. false	3. false	5. false
2. false	4. false	6. false

If you answered any of the above as TRUE, you need to read the following section very carefully!

1. *The rich have "secrets." I just need to learn them.* FALSE!

The secrets of the rich don't exist because the principles aren't a secret. The secrets to financial freedom may be difficult to DO, but they are NOT complicated to understand or implement.

Dozens, if not hundreds, of books and tape sets are offered each year to the public to help people "get rich quick." Most of them offer formulas that don't work, but they claim nonetheless to be revealing the "secrets of the rich." Trust me on this—the rich don't use secret information. They use tried-and-true, well-known principles related to working, saving, spending, and investing!

2. *I don't need to worry about retirement yet—I'll figure out something when I get to be that age.* FALSE!

I don't care what age you are, you should be concerned about retirement living. There's no shining knight headed your way on a white horse. Wake up! This is the real world where sad old people eat Alpo dog food, even in America. Don't be under the illusion that the government, which is highly inept and dim-witted when it comes to money management, is going to take great care of you in your golden years. Things will NOT be okay unless you make them that way. If you wait until you are sixty-five or seventy years old to "plan" for retirement, you will have missed the boat. Personally, I don't want to work at McDonald's when I retire, unless it's the one I own on St. Thomas in the U.S. Virgin Islands.

3. *I can get rich by working only a few hours a week, if I could just get trained and start selling the newest wonder product in a business I run out of my home.* FALSE!

I have never met a person who made a six-figure income by working just a few hours a week at ANYTHING. I recently received an e-mail from a man who offered me a 500-to-1 return on my money. I'm smart enough to know that 500-to-1 returns don't pan out. Anything that seems too good to be true . . . is.

Two of the hottest scams today are stuffing envelopes and doing medical billings from your home as ways to get rich. The truth is, envelopes are stuffed by machines at a rate of thousands a minute and at a cost of tenths of a penny. The only person getting rich off the envelope scam is the person selling you the "start-up kit." When it comes to medical billings, the legitimate, profitable medical biller is someone who works in the medical industry—not someone who takes a weekend course. The only person making money in that scam is the person who charged you for the course.

4. *I just need to learn how to buy and sell real-estate with "no money down" to get rich.* FALSE!

You can purchase real estate for nothing down, but then you owe so much on it there's no cash flow. You have to "feed" the project every month. I bought foreclosure and bankruptcy real estate for years and know it can be done, but the people with CASH are the ones who win, not the no-money-down people. The good deals are one in two hundred. The money is made by those who are experienced and very good at the business. I worked sixty hours a week in real estate, and it took me years to get to a six-figure income.

5. *I just need to find a way to get in on the tips related to hot stock deals.*

AND

6. *There's real money to be made in becoming my own "day-trader" stockbroker.* BOTH ARE FALSE!

The stock market attracts some of the brightest business minds on the planet. The really good brokers and analysts are those who study, track, chart, eat, and breathe the stock market for years, and sometimes generations. If you're going to be involved in the stock market, work with folks who have a good, LONG track record of success. You don't have time to climb the learning curve they've already climbed.

Exercise #25

The Gambler's Fantasy Land

There always seem to be those who just KNOW they are going to win at Lotto or some other form of gambling as a means of striking it rich. These people aren't living in denial as much as they are living in a fantasy world. Lotto is a rip-off—that's a hard, cold, mathematical, statistical fact.

Let's see what you really know about Lotto and similar institutional gaming programs:

1. The people who spend the most on Lotto and other gaming programs are:
   a. middle-class income earners
   b. lower-class income earners
   c. upper-class people who have money to waste

2. Lotto and other gaming programs are:
   a. hope-builders
   b. worth an occasional risk
   c. a tax on poor people

Answers:
1. (b.) The people who spend the most on Lotto and other gaming programs are lower-class income earners. Studies have shown the ZIP codes that spend four times what anyone else does are those in lower-income parts of town.

2. (c.) Lotto and other gaming programs are a tax on poor people. Gambling holds out false hope. The programs are based on dumb luck. Government-sponsored Lotto and other gaming programs are essentially a tax on the poor.

Key Concept #2

Get Smart About "Rich and Safe" Investments

There are a number of routinely offered investments that are based on a double-whammy of myths: Get rich, and be safe in the process. Among such investments are these:

- *Gold.* Many people believe gold is a good investment that will cover them if the economy collapses.
- *Whole-Life Insurance Policies.* Many people buy these policies expecting to retire wealthy.

What About You?

Do you own gold? Do you have a whole-life insurance policy? Do you know WHY these are lousy investments?

Exercise #26

Good with Gold?

How much do you REALLY know about investing in gold? Let's find out:

1. Gold is:
   a. a highly stable investment
   b. an investment every investor should have in his or her portfolio
   c. the standard used to exchange goods and services since the beginning of time
   d. all of the above
   e. none of the above

2. Gold is:

    a. the only thing that retains its value in a declining market

    b. the most secure investment

    c. the holder of the best long-term track record of all investments

    d. all of the above

    e. none of the above

Answers:
1 and 2: (e.) None of the above!

Gold is actually a lousy investment with a long track record of mediocrity. The average rates of return tracked as far back as Napoleon are around 2 percent gain per year. In the last fifty years, gold has had a record of around 4.4 percent gain a year, which is just about the same as inflation and just above the average passbook savings account. During that same time frame, an investor would have made an average of 12 percent in a good growth-stock mutual fund. During the past fifty years, gold has experienced extreme volatility as an investment and it is loaded with a great deal of risk.

Furthermore, gold is *not* used when economies fail. History shows that when an economy completely collapses the first thing that appears is a black-market barter system. In primitive cultures, items of utility often become the medium of exchange, and the same is temporarily true in a failed economy. A skill, a pair of blue jeans, or a tank of gas becomes very valuable—not gold coins or nuggets.

After a market collapse, one of the first things a new government establishes is paper money or coins.

Real estate, knowledge, and canned soup all are better hedges against a failed economy!

Exercise #27

Whole Life or Term Life?

Let's see what you know about whole-life insurance policies. Circle the choice (in capital letters) that you believe is correct. Note that cash-value policies include Whole Life, Universal Life, and Variable Life (which includes mutual funds). Whole-Life, Universal-Life, and most Cash-Value policies combine insurance and savings.

1. Cash-value insurance policies are **MORE / LESS** popular than term-life insurance policies.

2. The type of insurance that yields a higher payout upon death is **CASH-VALUE / TERM** life insurance.

3. The policy that costs you the most up front is **CASH-VALUE / TERM** life insurance.

Answers:

1. (MORE) Cash-value insurance policies are MORE popular than term-life insurance policies. Seventy percent of the life insurance policies sold today are cash-value policies.

2. (TERM) The type of insurance that yields a higher payout upon death is TERM life insurance (because you can afford the proper amount of coverage which is more insurance).

3. (CASH-VALUE) The policy that costs you the most up front is CASH-VALUE life insurance.

Have doubts or questions about the answers in this exercises? Let's do a little math exercise to illustrate:

Exercise #28

Leaving an Inheritance That
Includes Life Insurance Benefits

Bill, age thirty, has $100 a month to spend on life insurance. He shops the top five cash-value policy companies. How much life insurance can he purchase for his family with $100 a month?

   a. $125,000

   b. $250,000

   c. $1 million

   d. $75,000

Answer: (a.)

Joe, age thirty, wants to buy $125,000 worth of TERM life insurance. He will spend:

   a. $25 a month

   b. $75 a month

   c. $7 a month

   d. $40 a month

Answer: (c.)

Compare at this point: Bill is spending $100 a month for $125,000 in life insurance. Joe is spending $7 a month for $125,000 insurance.

"But," you say, "the $93 difference goes into a SAVINGS account for Bill so he has money during retirement." No, that's not entirely true.

For the first three years, the $93 goes to the insurance company for "expenses," including commissions. After that, the rate of return will average

- 2.6 percent a year for Whole Life
- *4.2 percent a year for Universal Life
- 7.4 percent a year for Variable Life (includes mutual funds)

(*These statistics are from *Consumer Reports,* the Consumer Federation of America, *Fortune* magazine, and *Kiplinger's Personal Finance.*)

With the Cash-Value policy purchased at $100 a month, the death benefit of a $125,000 policy that goes to Bill's family is:

    a. $125,000

    b. $200,000

    c. $400,000

    d. $500,000

Answer: (a.) Your family gets nothing that has accrued by interest. Your family gets only the $125,000, which is called the "face value" of the policy. The insurance company keeps your savings!

With the term policy purchased at $7 a month, the death benefit of a $125,000 policy that goes to Joe's family is:

    a. $125,000

    b. $100,000

    c. $200,000

    d. nothing

Answer: (a.) The benefit is the amount of the face value of the policy, in this example, $125,000.

If Joe had purchased a $125,000 term policy for $7 and put the extra $93 in a cookie jar, after three years his family would have $3,348 ($93 x 36 months) to INVEST. If Joe INVESTED the $93 over a twenty- to thirty-year term, he would have considerably more than Bill at retirement—far more if you add together death benefit and retirement funds!

PREVIEW: The Total Money Makeover plan presented later in this manual actually shows that by the time Joe reaches the age of fifty-seven, his kids will be grown and gone, and his house will be paid for. Joe will have invested $700,000 in mutual funds. At that point, he should become self-insured. Basically, by the time his term policy is "up," he won't NEED life insurance at all because he has no kids to feed and no house payment. His spouse will just have to suffer through with $700,000!

Key Concept #3

Get Smart About Real-Estate Investments

The best real-estate investment is a HOUSE—a single-family dwelling. There are lots of ways to save for a house and lots of ways to purchase a house. There's no substitute for owning a house as an investment!

Some people today are taking a "mobile home" route, thinking that owning a mobile home is the same as owning a house. It isn't. Trailers go down in value, not up.

What About You?

Quick—can you name the number one best real-estate investment?

Quick—tell me, is purchasing a mobile home a good INVESTMENT?

Exercise #29

Out at the Trailer Park

Let's do a little math on trailer-park investments:

1. Sue buys a $25,000 double-wide mobile home as an investment. At the end of five years:

    a. She will still owe $13,000 on the mobile home.

    b. She will still owe $22,000 on the mobile home.

    c. She will have paid for the mobile home in full.

2. Sue buys a $25,000 double-wide mobile home as an investment. At the end of five years, the mobile home will have a resale value of:

    a. $25,000

    b. $30,000 or more, assuming the real estate market is good

    c. $8,000

Answers:

1. (a.) After five years, Sue will have only about $3,000 equity in her mobile home.

2. (c.) After five years, Sue's initial $25,000 purchase will have a resale value of about $8,000.

The fact is, mobile homes go down in value almost as fast as cars do. They go down very quickly in value during the first five years. Few people want to own a five-year-old mobile home, at least not as an INVESTMENT property.

You may think I'm down on people who live in mobile homes. Not at all. I've lived in worse environments. But as an INVESTMENT, mobile homes are an unwise choice. The only time it might work is something I call "Ron's Rule," named after the man who told me what he had done.

Case Study: Ron

Ron and his wife sold their home for $120,000. They owed only $50,000 on it at the time, so they netted $70,000 on the deal. They used this money to pay CASH for a small farm and to buy a "very used" mobile home for $3,000, which they moved out to the farm. They lived in the mobile home while they worked and saved to build their dream home. Ron and his wife had a combined income of $85,000 a year. Ron was a contractor, and he was able to build their dream home for pennies on the dollar, so it didn't take long for them to earn and save enough to pay for their new home on a build-as-you-pay basis. When they moved into their new, debt-free home with an appraised value of $250,000, they sold the $3,000 mobile home for $3,200. The mobile home had lost virtually all its value by that time so the reselling came down to some clever negotiating on Ron's part.

Key Concept #4
Be Wise About "Prepaid" Investment Schemes

A number of schemes are basically founded on this idea: Pay now because you never know what it may cost in the future.

While it's true that you can't predict what it will cost in the future, these prepaid schemes rarely give a good rate of return. They are usually advertised as a "hedge against inflation," but, in fact, they don't provide much of a hedge.

Two of the most popular prepaid "hedge-against-inflation" schemes are those related to funeral expenses and college expenses.

If you prepay something, your return on the investment is basically the rate of inflation. For example, if you prepay college tuition, you will "save" only the difference between the amount tuition goes up between the time you lock into a rate and the time your child begins his college career. Since the inflation rate for tuition nationally has been about 7 percent a year, that's what your prepaid investment will return to you . . . about 7 percent. That's not bad, but mutual funds will average about 12 percent over a ten-year or longer time period. You'd be better off to take the amount you are dropping into a prepaid plan and invest it.

When it comes to funeral prepaying, I am a strong advocate for pre-PLANNING . . . but not pre-PAYING.

What About You?

Have you purchased a prepaid plan of any kind as a "hedge against infla-tion"? Did you honestly do the math with an independent financial coun-selor before making the purchase? If not, you have only yourself to blame.

Exercise #30

How Fancy a Funeral?

Sara's mom died suddenly, and in the midst of her intense grief, Sara felt she made unwise purchases as part of the funeral arrangements. She vowed not to leave her family in this predicament. So, at age thirty-nine, she prepaid $3,500 for a funeral.

If Sara had taken that same amount of money—$3,500—and invested it in a mutual fund that averaged 12 percent a year . . . and if she lived to age seventy-eight, her mutual fund would be worth:

    a. $50,000   d. $247,800

    b. $108,100   e. $358,500

    c. $173,300

Answer: (e.) Surely Sara could be buried for $358,500 with a little left over!

Pre-PLANNING, yes! For the cost of a little bit of paper and pencil lead, Sara could write a codicil to her will that voiced exactly what she wanted her family to purchase in the way of a casket, burial plot, and style of funeral. That would spare her family "decision-making anxiety" related to the funeral and burial.

Key Concept #5
Choose Wise Counsel When It Comes to Your Money

There's lots of advice available today on money management and estate planning. Make sure you get solid information!

DO take the time to work on a budget, retirement plan, and estate plan. In many ways, planning for your financial future is like planning for your future health. It's not a good idea to START exercising and eating right at age sixty-five if you want a healthy, high-quality life in your older years. It is a smart idea to start NOW and to do what is known to yield positive results, apart from any "fluke" situations such as accidents and massive outbreaks of plagues.

Get Professional Help

Do plan ahead. And do put your future money situation in the "IMPORTANT" category of priorities. You can pay the electric bill or sit in the dark on a month-to-month basis—there's a little flexibility when it comes to EXPENSES in retirement. But there aren't many options when it comes to monthly INCOME in retirement. That's the part you have to plan in advance.

Don't Turn to Debt-Management Companies

Don't count on debt-management companies to get you out of a problem—especially don't turn to ones that are highly advertised on television. It seems debt-management companies are springing up everywhere. They help you "manage" your debt by taking one monthly payment from you and distributing the money among your creditors, with whom they've often worked out lower payments and lower interest. This is NOT a loan, as with debt consolidation—some people get the two confused.

A company such as AmeriDebt or Consumer Credit Counseling Service may get you a better interest rate and a lower payment . . . but at a price. A huge hidden disadvantage is this: When you use one of these companies and then apply to get a Conventional, FHA, or VA loan, you will be treated the same as if you had filed for Chapter 13 Bankruptcy. Mortgage underwriting guidelines for traditional mortgages will put your credit in the "trashed" category. Especially don't take bankruptcy advice from debt-management companies. In all likelihood, you aren't bankrupt, you just need radical surgery on your finances.

You can't have somebody else diet for you or exercise for you and reap the health benefits. You have to change your habits and do these things for yourself if you truly want a physical fitness makeover. The same is true for money. You can't have someone else "manage" your habits and see true change.

Say "No" to Credit Cleanup Companies

Only inaccuracies in reporting or posting on credit reports can be "cleaned up." Misdeeds related to poor spending habits cannot be washed away. This isn't my opinion. It's the law.

The Federal Fair Credit Reporting Act dictates how consumers and creditors interact with the credit bureaus. Bad credit drops off a credit report after seven years, unless you have a Chapter 7 Bankruptcy, which stays on for ten years. If you have inaccuracies that need to be removed, there's a form at the back of this book to use.

Some of the so-called "cleanup" companies are actually engaging in fraud. One company offers a "kit" for $300—it tells you to dispute all bad credit and have it removed even if the item was reported accurately. Don't do that. It's fraud, and you can be arrested and jailed! Some of these companies recommend you get a new Social Security number. By getting a second identity, you get a brand-new credit report and lenders won't discover your past misdeed. This is also fraud. In essence, you are lying to get a loan. That is a criminal act.

Be Wary of "Collectors" Who Operate as "Middlemen"

Any deal, special plan, or settlement you make with a middleman "bill collector" must be in WRITING, and the written agreement must be BEFORE you send any money. NEVER allow collectors electronic access to your checking account. NEVER send postdated checks. If a collector abuses you after you've given them access to your account or sent a postdated check, there is nothing you can do—because you owe them money.

NOTE: At the end of this chapter you will find sample copies of letters and other information related to CREDIT BUREAUS.

What About You?

If your best friend asked you what to do about "debt problems," where would you tell that person to turn?

Simple Q & A

Q: According to the *Wall Street Journal,* there are over _____ Sears cards with more than 700,000 new applications per month.

A: 63 million

Exercise #31

Putting a Priority on Planning

How much time did you spend this past month managing a retirement plan, 401k, Roth IRA, or some other vehicle—reading up on investments and reading your portfolio statements, purchasing CDs, or conducting any other business related to the income you hope to have twenty years from now? _____ hours

Check ALL the items below that you spent more time doing this past month:

- ❏ Shopping for clothes
- ❏ Going to movies
- ❏ Washing the car
- ❏ Mowing the lawn
- ❏ Shopping for beauty or makeup products
- ❏ Talking to neighbors over the back fence
- ❏ Watching soap operas
- ❏ Watching sports programs on TV
- ❏ Window-shopping
- ❏ Gossiping on the phone with a friend
- ❏ Browsing through catalogs
- ❏ Waiting idly in a waiting room (or transportation terminal or lounge)
- ❏ Sitting in a bar by yourself
- ❏ Watching TV game shows and sitcoms
- ❏ Reading junk mail
- ❏ Cruising through the shops at the mall
- ❏ Watching infomercials
- ❏ Waiting to be seated at a restaurant

The activities listed in Exercise #31 are all highly "temporary" and "passing" in nature. None of them produce ANYTHING that will last twenty years or that increases a person's net worth.

Key Concept #6
Know Who Owes

Some people are ignorant about what they owe and don't owe. Sadly, this is often the case when it comes to debt and divorce. A divorce decree may say your spouse has to pay the debt, BUT divorce decrees do not have the power to take your name off credit cards and mortgages, so if your spouse doesn't pay, be ready to. You still owe the debt. If your spouse doesn't pay, you can report the lack of payment to the judge, but you are still liable for the debt. A lender who doesn't get paid will correctly report bad credit on ALL parties to the loan (or charge card), and a lender can correctly sue the parties to the loan (or charge card).

If you are going to leave a marriage, make sure that all debts are refinanced out of your name, or force the sale of the item.

Exercise #32

Know Who Pays for What

Identify the statements below as true or false.

TRUE FALSE

❏ ❏   1. If both you and your husband signed for the loan to buy his truck, and he gets the truck in a divorce settlement but he doesn't make payments on the truck after your divorce, the truck may be repossessed by the lender, and YOU may be sued for the balance still owed on the vehicle.

TRUE FALSE

❏   ❏   2. If you quitclaim-deed your ownership in the family home to your wife as part of a property settlement, and she doesn't make payments on time, YOUR credit may be trashed.

❏   ❏   3. Even if your husband pays on the truck, or your wife pays on the house in a timely manner, YOU may have difficulty qualifying for your next home loan because you "have too much debt" related to that item you no longer own or use.

Answers:

1. true
2. true
3. true

Sad, but very true.

Exercise #33

*Bankruptcy Doesn't
Mean It's "Over Over"*

Filing bankruptcy and "starting over" is made to sound so easy on the television commercials. The fact is, bankruptcy is a gut-wrenching, life-changing event that can cause lifelong damage. People who file bankruptcy often feel beaten up, beaten down, and deserted . . . but some who file bankruptcy are far from bankrupt. Unless you are truly bankrupt, don't ever think bankruptcy is an easy way out. Let's see what you truly know about bankruptcy:

1. Bankruptcy:

   a. is one of the top five life-altering NEGATIVE events a person can experience.

   b. is only temporary.

   c. doesn't impact your future job applications.

   d. won't impact a loan application if you wait several years to apply for the loan.

2. When it comes to bankruptcy:

   a. Most bankruptcies can be avoided.

   b. There are ways to make bankruptcy "pain-free."

   c. Bankruptcy is the "quick fix" that makes life easier.

Answers:

1. (a.) Bankruptcy is one of the top five life-altering NEGATIVE events a person can experience.

Bankruptcy is ranked right up there with divorce, severe illness, disability, and the loss of a loved one when it comes to negative stress and impact. I personally don't think it's equal to the loss of a loved one, but the wounds are deep to both a person's psyche and a person's credit report.

Bankruptcy is not temporary. Its effects linger for a lifetime. Many job applications, and virtually all loan applications from legitimate lenders, ask if you have *ever* filed for bankruptcy. If you lie to get a loan because your bankruptcy is very old, you are still committing fraud. You have committed a criminal act, and you may be prosecuted for it.

2. (a.) When it comes to bankruptcy, most bankruptcies can be avoided.

The vast majority of bankruptcies don't need to occur. Radical changes may be required by the person who is deeply in debt, but bankruptcy very often can be avoided. It should be viewed only as a last resort. There are NO ways to make bankruptcy "pain-free." It is never a "quick fix" that results in an easier life. It's a giant step backward in a person's quest for financial freedom.

Key Concept #7

Carry Cash

Carrying cash is the most powerful key I know to controlling your spending habits. People are highly reluctant to "part with" the cash in their wallet or purse. They will toss a credit card onto the counter in a heartbeat but agonize over pulling out a $20 bill to pay for lunch.

One of the biggest excuses I hear for not carrying cash is, "I might get robbed." You might. I'm not making light of crime. But are you aware that there are crooks who specialize in taking credit cards? Not only for the use of them, but as a tool for ripping off your total financial identity? And that's not even applying the label "crooks" to those who issue credit cards and take your money at extremely high interest rates when you don't pay for your credit-card charges within thirty days!

What About You?

How much money do you have in your wallet? How many credit cards to you have? Which are you likely to reach for first? Why?

Exercise #34

Carrying Cash

In a culture in which people think only drug dealers carry cash, you may find this "key concept" a little weird. Cash, however, is powerful. If you carry cash, several things happen. Let's see if you can anticipate what they are.

Circle the number associated with every item on the next page that you believe statistical reports have shown to be TRUE about going to a cash-only spending policy:

1. People spend less as a whole.

2. People get better bargains (by negotiating discounts).

3. It is easier to gain control of out-of-control spending habits.

4. It is easier to budget.

5. It is easier to say no to impulse buying.

6. It is easier to keep track of "how much is left" in a particular category of a family budget.*

(* This strategy relates to those who divide their cash into envelopes for items such as "groceries," "entertainment," "personal beauty products," and so forth. The cash is allocated to envelopes as part of a budgeting process. When an envelope is out of cash, there's no more to be spent that month in that category!)

Answers:

All the above numbers should be circled. Cash-only spending helps in every one of these ways.

Key Concept #8
*Maintain Basic
Insurance Policies*

You may have concluded from a previous section on life insurance that I am opposed to insurance of all kinds. Not so! I believe every person should have these basics:

- Health insurance
- Auto insurance
- Homeowners insurance
- Life insurance (if you are married or have children)
- Long-term disability insurance
- Long-term care insurance (if you are over age sixty)

When it comes to the "payout" of a life insurance policy, be sure to specify in a will how you want the money disbursed. Some people seem to believe that if they make a will, they will die. The truth is, you ARE going to die. It's far better for your loved ones if you die with a will in place than if you die without one.

Exercise #35

Insurance Savvy

Let's see how sharp you are when it comes to getting the most for your money in the insurance world:

1. A good strategy for saving on auto and homeowners insurance is:
   a. Choose higher deductibles to save on premiums.
   b. Pay for only about two-thirds of what the agent tells you is full-replacement value.
   c. Pay in installment plans rather than once or twice a year.
   d. All of the above.

2. When purchasing life insurance:
   a. Buy a cash-value policy instead of term insurance.
   b. Buy a policy that will help you "save for retirement."
   c. Buy a twenty-year term policy equal to two times your annual income.
   d. Buy a twenty-year term policy equal to ten times your annual income.

3. When considering long-term disability insurance:
   a. Recognize that if you are thirty-two years old, you are twelve times more likely to become disabled than to die by age sixty-five.
   b. Buy this type of insurance through your employer if you can, usually at a fraction of the cost otherwise.
   c. Get coverage that equals 50 to 70 percent of your annual income.

    d. All of the above.

    e. None of the above.

4. Health insurance is:

    a. the number-one cause of bankruptcy filings when you don't have enough.

    b. one area where you definitely do not want a high deductible.

    c. impossible to get if you are self-employed.

    d. not related to any of the above.

5. Long-term care insurance:

    a. covers in-home care or nursing home care.

    b. works only in nursing homes.

    c. should be purchased by any person over age sixty, regardless of their net worth.

    d. both a and c are correct.

Answers:

1. (a.) A good strategy for saving on auto and homeowners insurance is to choose higher deductibles to save on premiums. I don't recommend underinsuring and, besides, the companies will not do that anymore. Paying in installment plans is more expensive because there are processing fees associated with each payment.

2. (d.) When purchasing life insurance buy a twenty-year term policy equal to ten times your annual income. This is the best option until you reach the point in your mutual fund investments where you don't need life insurance to support your family.

3. (d.) When considering long-term disability insurance, recognize that if you are thirty-two years old, you are twelve times more likely to become disabled than to die by age sixty-five. Buy this type of insurance through your employer if you can, usually at a fraction of the cost otherwise, and get coverage that equals 50 to 70 percent of your annual income.

4. (a.) A lack of health insurance is the number one cause of bankruptcy filings. Stated another way, the number one cause of bankruptcy is medical bills that cannot be paid. (The number two cause is out-of-control credit-card debt.) If you are in good health and have a good income, choose a large deductible to lower your premium. If you are self-employed, look for an MSA (Medical Savings Account) plan. It will help you save on premiums and taxes.

5. (d.) Long-term care insurance covers in-home care or nursing home care, and it should be purchased by any person over age sixty regardless of their net worth. The average nursing home stay can easily cost $40,000 a year, and that's not counting extra medical services that might be required for extreme-care cases. That amount can gobble up an investment portfolio very quickly.

Exercise #36

How Much Insurance?

How much life insurance should you have? You need about ten times your annual income. Invested at 10 percent, the return on this investment would produce an income to cover the need.

What is ten times your current annual income? $_____

*Approximate Term Insurance Costs:**
Age 30: $.60 per $1,000 coverage
Age 40: $.90 per $1,000 coverage
Age 50: $2.50 per $1,000 coverage
Age 60: $6.65 per $1,000 coverage
(*These figures are estimated for a twenty-year term policy. Tobacco users add 100 percent.)

Here's the very basic formula for calculating how much you need:

Primary: _____ (thousands desired) x _____ (rate per $1,000) = $ _____

Secondary:_____ (thousands desired) x _____ (rate per $1,000) = $ _____

   Add together for TOTAL MONTHLY PREMIUM: $ _____

(NOTE: An insurance-coverage recap form is located at the end of this chapter. Keep this in your file of IMPORTANT PAPERS. Continually check term policies against the open market prices with an independent agent because term prices are dropping steadily.)

Exercise #37

Making a Will

Let's see how much you know about estate planning:

1 Estate planners report that _____ percent of Americans die without a will.

   a. 15

   b. 30

   c. 50

   d. 70

2. If you don't have a written will that's properly prepared:

   a. There's no assurance your estate will be disbursed in the way you want.

   b. The "state" will dictate how your estate will be divided.

   c. Your estate may end up in probate (the court system's means of dealing with undesignated estates) for years, which means attorneys may be the primary beneficiaries.

   d. Your children and spouse will automatically get what you have in equal amounts.

   e. Answers a, b, and c, but not d.

3. The Bible says, "A good man leaves _____ to his children's children" (Prov. 13:22).

   a. A spiritual blessing
   b. A house
   c. An inheritance
   d. A Bible

Answers:

1. (d.) Estate planners report that 70 percent of Americans die without a will. Sad, but true. That means the vast majority of people do not die with a will in place. That's sheer stupidity.

2. (e.) If you don't have a written will that's properly prepared, there's no assurance your estate will be disbursed in the way you want. The state will dictate how your estate will be divided. Your estate may end up in probate (the court system's means of dealing with undesignated estates) for years, which means attorneys may be the primary beneficiaries. There is NO guarantee your children and spouse will automatically get what you have in equal amounts.

   In other words, if you don't have a will that is properly prepared and executed, there's no telling how things will end up. Generally speaking, the government will get far more than you intended, and your children and spouse may be left in need.

3. (c.) The Bible says, "A good man leaves AN INHERITANCE to his children's children" (Prov. 13:22). Certainly you should leave your children a good spiritual heritage and family legacy, but also leave your children a good inheritance. It's a sign you love them enough to care about their future welfare. As far as I'm concerned, we each should go out with style and plenty in the bank.

---------------------- 5 ----------------------

Sailing Over Two More Hurdles: IGNORANCE and KEEPING UP WITH THE JONESES

Key Concept #1

There's a Price to Be Paid for Financial Freedom

We each must identify the hurdles we'll face if we are to win the battle against overspending and financial mismanagement. If you don't identify the hurdles, you'll just keep tripping over them. If you are in denial about whether you have a financial problem . . . face up to reality. If you have bought into myths about debt, or believe that debt is the way to become wealthy, wake up and admit you've been conned. If you have believed the myths about money that are often perpetuated by our culture, choose instead to now believe the truth about money.

If you are seeking to become physically fit and you have a major problem when it comes to eating Ben & Jerry's ice cream, you should tell your trainer before you try to change your diet and exercise program. You must admit you have an ice cream problem and recognize the myths about ice cream as a great weight-loss food. Then and only then can you proceed with healthful eating and exercise in order to change your habits and thus your fitness level.

I encourage you to keep in mind the statement made by the great philosopher Pogo, as published years ago in the Sunday comics: "We have met the enemy and he is us."

What About You?

What do YOU see as the hurdles that stand between where you are NOW in your finances and true FINANCIAL FREEDOM?

Exercise #38

Identifying the Hurdles

List three to five hurdles you see standing between you and the day when you truly can say, "I'm financially fit and free." Define "financially fit and free" as being able to make choices about how you want to live, give, and invest quickly and without strain. Define "financially fit and free" as the day when you are able to live off the interest on your investments. What are the hurdles?

1. _____

2. _____

3. _____

4. _____

5. _____

Key Concept #2

*Choose to Become
Financially Smart*

Ignorance is a major hurdle when it comes to handling money. I hope you identified it as a hurdle above, because most hurdles cannot be overcome without some new knowledge. No one is born financially smart. Each of us has to learn how to deal wisely with money. Don't be defensive about this. Ignorance is not a lack of intelligence—it's a lack of know-how.

I've met a lot of babies in my life, but I've never seen a baby who was born ready to handle wealth. Just as nobody is born with the knowledge to drive a car, no one is born with a "financial gene" that enables him or her to manage the $2 million that person may very well make in a lifetime (either individually or as partner in a marriage).

What About You?

How much do you know about the way the truly rich—as in, financially solvent and beyond bill-juggling into wealth building—live and manage money? Do you believe you are financially "smart" or "dumb"?

Exercise #39

How Do the Rich Live?

How do you believe millionaires live? Let's see if you truly know. Indicate whether you believe the statements below are true or false:

TRUE FALSE

❑ ❑   1. Millionaires usually live in big houses.

❑ ❑   2. Millionaires usually drive new cars.

❑ ❑   3. Millionaires usually wear designer clothes.

❑ ❑   4. Millionaires have a high need for approval and respect from others.

❑ ❑   5. Millionaires rarely look for bargains or sales.

❑ ❑   6. Millionaires are more motivated by a goal of financial security than by peer pressure.

Answers:
1. false
2. false
3. false
4. false
5. false
6. true

In response to statements 1–5: Dr. Tom Stanley, author of *The Millionaire Next Door,* found in his study of millionaires that most millionaires live in middle-class houses, drive paid-for cars that are two years old or older, and are just as likely to buy blue jeans at a discount store as fancy clothes. Millionaires are very bargain-conscious, and they frequently wait for items to go on sale.

In response to statement 6: Millionaires are INFINITELY more motivated by the goal of financial security than by what their friends and family members think of them.

Key Concept #3

Stop Trying to Keep Up with the Joneses

Peer pressure, cultural expectations, attaining a "reasonable standard of living," keeping up with the Joneses (whoever they are)—I don't care how you phrase it, we all struggle with a desire to be accepted by our family, friends, and peers. We seek approval and respect. This desire sometimes drives us to do rather insane things.

Now, I'm not at all opposed to LEARNING from the Joneses—if the Joneses are truly succeeding financially. Actually, I'm all in favor of that!

If you want to become thin and muscular, you need to study the habits of people who are thin and muscular. If you want to be rich, you should study the habits and value systems of the rich.

What About You?

Are you living in denial today about your financial state or your financial future? Are you living in a FALSE sense of security? Let's find out . . .

Case Study: Bob and Sara

Bob and Sara make $93,000 a year and have done so for the last seven years. What do they have to show for their earnings? They live in a $400,000 home, but they still owe $390,000 on it. This amount includes a home-equity loan they took out on the house to purchase furniture. They have two $30,000 cars that are leased. They have $52,000 in credit-card debt. They travel often and are dressed in high-fashion clothes. They still owe $25,000 on a student loan from college, which is now ten years old. On the positive side, they have $2,000 in savings and $18,000 in a retirement fund (401k).

Bob and Sara LOOK very good. Bob's mother is impressed with their lifestyle, and Sara's brother frequently stops by to ask for money because he says "you obviously are doing well." They present a perfect picture.

But . . . Bob and Sara have a negative net worth! Behind their perfect hairdos and French manicures, they have a growing sense of desperation and futility, their marriage is unraveling around the edges, and they are feeling disgusted with themselves.

Now, if Bob and Sara each weighed five hundred pounds, people might look at them and conclude: *They're too fat. They need to lose weight, or their health is going to suffer.* But because Bob and Sara have an "over-weight" problem in their finances, nobody can see the problem, and they continue to appear cool, even though, technically, they are broke. They need to get rid of the cars, sell their house, and move into a house and drive cars they can afford.

Why don't Bob and Sara make this change? Because they LIKE their nice house and nice cars, and trading them for something less would be painful to their pride.

Owning up to the fact that you are a financial fake takes tremendous courage. It is hard to admit to yourself, much less to family members and friends, that you really aren't doing as well as you APPEAR to be doing.

Exercise #40

Are You a Financial Fake?

Circle your honest answer associated with each of the statements below.

1. I would find it VERY painful to admit to friends that I can't really afford to go out with them to a fancy, expensive restaurant. I'd make up some other excuse besides money.

   YES   NO

2. I don't believe I could admit to my family that I can't afford to buy every person a Christmas gift this year.

   YES   NO

3. I would be embarrassed to trade in my luxury car for an older, used car, even though I struggle with making car payments every month.

   YES   NO

4. I would NOT go to see a financial counselor about my budget—word might get around that I needed financial help.

   YES   NO

5. I KNOW I need to make some financial changes, but I just can't seem to bring myself to make them.

   YES   NO

6. I sometimes lie awake at night, wondering and even worrying about how I'm going to pay for the things I have without making any changes in my overall lifestyle.

   YES   NO

7. I would find it very embarrassing to move from our current home into a "less ritzy" neighborhood.

   YES   NO

8. I have to admit that I seem to owe more in credit-card charges every month, but I truly don't know what I purchase that is increasingly expensive.

   YES   NO

9. I like the reputation I have as a "Shopping Queen" (or "Shopping King").

   YES   NO

10. I don't just want to keep up with the Joneses—I want to BE the Joneses that others try to keep up with.

    YES   NO

Answers:

If you answered YES to any of the above, you need to recognize that you need to address an attitude-adjustment issue before you will ever be able to do what is necessary to achieve financial freedom or build genuine wealth.

Case Study: Dave

My weak spot is cars. After starting with nothing and becoming a millionaire the first time by age twenty-six, I had the eye of my heart set on a Jaguar. I "needed" a Jaguar. What I really needed was for people to be impressed with my success. What I needed was for my family to raise its collective eyebrow of approval. What I yearned for was respect. What I was so shallow to believe was that the car I drove gave me those things.

God used the whole going broke story to give my heart a Total Money Makeover in the area of peer pressure.

As I was going broke and losing everything, I kept the Jaguar by refinancing it repeatedly at different, "friendlier" banks. I even went so far as to get a good friend to co-sign a loan so I could keep this image car. I couldn't afford to keep up the maintenance on the car, so it began to deteriorate. It ran poorly and wasn't reliable, but I still loved it and hung on. Within the year of our bankruptcy, we were so broke that our electricity was once cut off for two days. I have often wondered what the guy from the electric company thought as he stood in the driveway next to my Jaguar and pulled my electric meter. My behavior was sick.

The car continued to deteriorate, and the main seal on the oil pan cracked. This caused oil coming out the back of the engine onto the muffler to burn. The burning oil, lots of it, created a smoke screen for miles behind me everywhere I went. The bid to fix it was $1,700 and I hadn't seen an extra $1,700 in months, so I just kept driving my James Bond smoke-screen mobile.

Finally, my friend got really tired of making the payments he had co-signed for and gently suggested I sell my precious car. I was so mad at him! How dare he suggest that I sell my car! So he quit making the payments, and the bank not so gently suggested I sell the car or they would repo it. I tried to stall and only came to my senses and sold the Jaguar on a Thursday morning because the bank assured me they would take it on Friday.

I was able to work my way through the mess and pay back the bank and even my friend, but the process was humiliating. Because I was too stubborn to address what that car represented in my life, I caused much damage that was avoidable.

God began to heal the weak spot in my heart that was desperate for peer and family approval. I became so disgusted with myself when I realized the depth of my stupidity about that Jaguar that I went into "abstinence"—meaning I didn't care what we drove or what it looked like as long as we were winning in our Total Money Makeover.

There's an interesting footnote to all this. Fifteen years later, we had become wealthy again, and I decided to get a different car. By that time I had become firmly entrenched in looking for a one- or two-year-old car. I pay cash for my cars. I am always looking for a DEAL. A friend in the car business called me one day with a deal . . . on a Jaguar. All those years and tears later—when driving a Jaguar no longer was the driving force behind my desire for a "high approval rating"—God sent a Jaguar back into my life. But He did so only when a Jaguar was no longer my idol. Rumor has it that God doesn't like us to have other gods in our lives.

Exercise #41

What's Your Image?

How important to you are the items below when it comes to your "Image"?

(1) Not Important	(2) Somewhat Important	(3) Fairly Important	(4) Very Important

1. Pulling out a "gold" or platinum credit card to pay for dinner: ____

2. Having someone compliment you on the brand of watch you wear: ____

3. Having someone notice that you are wearing designer clothing: ____

4. Having someone comment on how nice a neighborhood you live in: ____

5. Having someone say about your automobile, "I'd love to have a car like that someday": ____

6. Noticing that other people are noticing that you are wearing expensive shoes: ____

7. Being seen at the high-priced benefit dinner or cocktail party: ___

8. Picking up the tab at dinner (even if you can't really afford to do so): ___

9. Accepting an invitation to go on a vacation trip that's over your budget: ___

10. Being the person about whom others say, "He's really doing well": ___

Exercise #42

About Those Joneses . . .

One simple question as we conclude this segment of the workbook: Have you made a decision not to keep up with the Joneses?

YES   NO

The fact is, by now you should be realizing that the Joneses:
   a. may not be as "rich" as they appear to be.
   b. no longer live next door because they got wise and moved to a neighborhood they could afford.
   c. are broke.

Answer:
Any of these answers will do, but I especially like answer "c."
As for the **YES / NO** question . . . I trust your answer is YES.

Key Concept #4
*Decide Before the Climb If You
Are Willing to Follow the Guide*

Just by the sheer fact that you have worked through this workbook to get to this page, I assume that you have faced up to and are addressing some of the areas in your financial life that may have been "blind spots" up to now. It's as if you are standing at the bottom of a mountain and you suddenly have a clear view of the top. You feel ready to climb.

Simple Q & A

Q: *Ladies Home Journal* has reported that more than _____ offers of credit cards go to each household in America each year.

A: forty-three

One thing I've learned through the years as I have sought to lose fat and become more physically in shape is this: Things that once required great physical output from me are now easier. I believe that is also true for those who have busted through denial, climbed over debt myths, scaled the wall of money myths, and are working through ignorance and the pride-based competitive desire to keep up with the Joneses. Doing the RIGHT things become easier.

What About You?

As you climb the mountain toward financial security and freedom, there is a distinct and clear path that takes a person to the top. The good thing about this path is that it is not virgin territory. It is narrow, but many people have walked it. The climb is hard, but it takes a person to the summit.

In the valley below is the well-beaten interstate with millions of people traveling on it. The interstate takes a person in any one of a thousand scattered destinations, none of which offer a clear view of financial freedom or fitness.

What do you want?

Exercise #43

Rule of Thumb

Fill in the blank below. Those who have completed a twelve-step program probably will get this answer immediately. The phrase is common to recovery programs:

Continuing to do the same thing over and over again, and expecting a different result, is the definition of _____ .

Answer: INSANITY

6

Walk Before You Run:
SAVE $1,000

Key Concept #1

Proceed One Step at a Time . . . but Keep Walking

One of my favorite older movies is the comedy *What About Bob?* starring Bill Murray. The therapist in that movie had written a book titled *Baby Steps,* and the framework for the movie is this statement: "You can get anywhere if you simply go one step at a time." I believe that's true for walking the path to financial freedom.

We certainly know that to be true in the fitness world. Exercise gurus are quick to say, "Start where you are . . . but do start." Do what you can do and then next week, do just a little more. Take it slow, and you won't be discouraged, but you will see progress. If you wake up one morning and realize you need to lose a hundred pounds, build up your cardiovascular system, and tone your muscles, you might be tempted to quit eating, run three miles that morning, and lift every weight you can lift to work out every muscle group in your body . . . and you'd probably collapse. If you didn't collapse during the workout, you'd probably collapse forty-eight hours later when your muscle groups locked up.

When it comes to financial fitness, the same is true. If you try to do everything at once, your progress will seem very slow, and you'll likely become discouraged and give up. I never recommend that people put 3 percent in their 401k, $50 extra on every house payment, and $5 extra on every credit card payment—to do that dilutes the effort and nothing seems doable.

The steps I offer you in the Total Money Makeover are in a particular sequence for a reason. Don't skip ahead. Start with Baby Step One, saving $1,000, and move through the rest of them. If you try to shortcut the process, you are much more prone to failure. The same is true if you try to take the steps in a different sequence. Remember, this is a tried-and-true path to the top. I've counseled tens of thousands of people up this mountain, and the path takes you there, if you stick to the path!

Before you take Baby Step One, you need to set up a budget. Make that a Written . . . Comprehensive . . . New budget—every month.

Your budget is your blueprint in building the House of Success. If you don't tell money what to do in a budget, it "leaves."

What About You?

Do you have a written budget for THIS month? Commit yourself to making one now!

Exercise #44

Balance Your Checkbook

Before you can make a budget, you must have a balanced checkbook so you know how much you have and where it's at. This exercise is up to you—find your checkbook and balance it.

NOTE: If you need help, see the pages that follow on "How to Balance Your Checkbook" and the example sheet for reconciling your bank balance. That sheet is labeled "Bank Balance Example." Don't proceed until you have done this!

How to Balance Your Checkbook

Keep your checkbook register current by subtracting both checks and withdrawals and adding deposits, as they're made, to keep your checkbook balanced correctly.

Balance your checkbook within 72 hours of receiving your bank statement (to make sure there aren't any mistakes).

What do I need to balance my checkbook?

1. Your checkbook register
2. Your last bank statement
3. A reconciliation sheet (located on the back of most statements)

Where do I start?   Checkbook vs. Bank Statement

Start by putting check marks, in your checkbook, for each of the checks and deposits included in your bank statement. Make an entry in your checkbook for any bank service charges (or interest paid) made by the bank.

Checkbook Register						
Check Number	**Date**	**Fee**	**Transaction Description**	**Payment**	**Deposit**	**Balance** $564.46
5671	8/12	x	One-Stop Grocery	57.40		507 06
5672	8/14		Electric Company	101.00		406 06
	8/14		Paycheck		700.00	1106 06
5673	8/16		Telephone Company	50.00		1056 06
5674	8/19		One-Stop Grocery	66.00		990 06
		X	Bank Service Charge	2.50		987 56

Bank Balance Example

On the reconciliation sheet, list any checks and/or withdrawals or other deductions that are in your checkbook that are not on your bank statement, then total the list.

On the reconciliation sheet, list any deposits that are in your checkbook but are not included on your bank statement, then total the list.

Beginning with the ending balance from your bank statement, subtract the total withdrawals, then add the total deposits that were not on your statement.

Compare with your checkbook balance. If they don't agree, double-check your lists, then re-add your checkbook entries until you find the difference.

List the balance from your bank statement $ 504.56

List the checks from your checkbook that aren't on your statement

The Electric Company	5672	8/14	101 00
Telephone Company	5673	8/16	50 00
One-Stop Grocery	5674	8/19	66 00

TOTAL $ 217 00   (-) $ 217.00

List the deposit amounts in your checkbook that aren't on your statement

Pay Check	8/14		700 00

TOTAL $ 700 00   (+) $ 700.00

This should be your checkbook balance $ 987.56

Exercise #45

A Basic Quickie Budget

There are several forms on the following pages for you to complete or use as you make a basic monthly budget.

Follow these basic rules:

- Every dollar of your income should be allocated to some category on a budget. Money "left over" should be put back in a category, even if you make up a new category. You are making the spending decisions ahead of time here. Almost every category (except debt) should have some dollar amount in it.

- Initially, your "savings" will go to building up an emergency fund. Later, this "savings" money needs to be allocated to items that need periodic replacement. Example: If you do not plan to replace the furniture, when you do replace it, you will cause strain by borrowing, so go ahead and plan now by saving for new furniture. I have actually had people tell me they can do without clothing. Oh, COME ON! Be careful in your zeal to make the numbers work that you don't substitute the urgent for the important.

- Fill in the amount for each subcategory under "Subtotal" and then the total for each main category under "Total." As you go through your first month, fill in the "Actually Spent" column with your real expenses or the saving you did for that area. If there is a substantial difference in the plan versus the reality, something has to give. Either you will have to adjust the amount allocated to that area up another area down, or you will have to control your spending in that area.

- The line "Percent of Take-Home Pay" is the percentage of take-home pay that category represents; for example, what percentage of your total take-home pay do you spend on "Housing"? Compare that to the chart labeled "Recommended Percentages." You may need to consider adjusting your lifestyle!

BASIC QUICKIE BUDGET

GET STARTED TODAY ON MAKING A DIFFERENCE IN YOUR FINANCIAL FUTURE

Item	Monthly Total	Payoff Total	How far Behind	Type Account
GIVING	_____	_____	_____	_____
SAVING	_____		_____	_____
HOUSING				
First Mortgage	_____	_____	_____	_____
Second Mortgage	_____	_____	_____	_____
Repairs/Mn. Fee	_____		_____	_____
UTILITIES				
Electricity	_____		_____	_____
Water	_____		_____	_____
Gas	_____		_____	_____
Phone	_____		_____	_____
Trash	_____		_____	_____
Cable	_____		_____	_____
*FOOD	_____		_____	_____
TRANSPORTATION				
Car Payment	_____	_____	_____	_____
Car Payment	_____	_____	_____	_____
*Gas & Oil	_____		_____	_____
*Repairs & Tires	_____		_____	_____
Car Insurance	_____		_____	_____
*CLOTHING	_____		_____	_____
PERSONAL				
Disability Ins.	_____		_____	_____
Health Insurance	_____		_____	_____
Life Insurance	_____		_____	_____
Child Care	_____		_____	_____
*Entertainment	_____		_____	_____
OTHER MISC.	_____		_____	_____
TOTAL MONTHLY NECESSITIES	_____			

*Use the envelope system for these expenses.

INCOME SOURCES

SOURCE	AMOUNT	PERIOD / DESCRIBE
Salary 1	$1,700	1st & 15th - $850
Salary 2	$1,300	2 WEEKS - $650
Salary 3		
Bonus		
Self-Employment		
Interest Income		
Dividend Income		
Royalty Income		
Rents		
Notes		
Alimony		
Child Support		
AFDC		
Unemployment		
Social Security		
Pension		
Annuity		
Disability Income		
Cash Gifts		
Trust Fund		
Other _____		
Other _____		
Other _____		
TOTAL	$3,000	

INCOME SOURCES

SOURCE	AMOUNT	PERIOD / DESCRIBE
Salary 1	_____	_____
Salary 2	_____	_____
Salary 3	_____	_____
Bonus	_____	_____
Self-Employment	_____	_____
Interest Income	_____	_____
Dividend Income	_____	_____
Royalty Income	_____	_____
Rents	_____	_____
Notes	_____	_____
Alimony	_____	_____
Child Support	_____	_____
AFDC	_____	_____
Unemployment	_____	_____
Social Security	_____	_____
Pension	_____	_____
Annuity	_____	_____
Disability Income	_____	_____
Cash Gifts	_____	_____
Trust Fund	_____	_____
Other _____	_____	_____
Other _____	_____	_____
Other _____	_____	_____
TOTAL	_____	_____

LUMP-SUM PAYMENT PLANNING

Payments you make on a NON-monthly basis can be budget busters if not planned for, so we are converting them to a monthly basis for you to use on the "Monthly Cash-Flow Plan" sheet where you will set money aside monthly to avoid strain or borrowing when these events occur. If an item here is already paid monthly, enter NA. If you make a payment quarterly, then annualize it for this sheet.

ITEM NEEDED	ANNUAL AMOUNT		MONTHLY AMOUNT
Real Estate Taxes		/ 12 =	
Homeowners Insurance		/ 12 =	
Home Repairs		/ 12 =	
Replace Furniture	$600	/ 12 =	$50
Medical Bills		/ 12 =	
Health Insurance		/ 12 =	
Life Insurance		/ 12 =	
Disability Insurance		/ 12 =	
Car Insurance		/ 12 =	
Car Repair/Tags		/ 12 =	
Replace Car		/ 12 =	
Clothing		/ 12 =	
Tuition		/ 12 =	
Bank Note		/ 12 =	
IRS (Self-Employed)		/ 12 =	
Vacation	$1,800	/ 12 =	$150
Gifts (incl. Christmas)	$1,200	/ 12 =	$100
Other _____		/ 12 =	

LUMP-SUM PAYMENT PLANNING

Payments you make on a NON-monthly basis can be budget busters if not planned for, so we are converting them to a monthly basis for you to use on the "Monthly Cash-Flow Plan" sheet where you will set money aside monthly to avoid strain or borrowing when these events occur. If an item here is already paid monthly, enter NA. If you make a payment quarterly, then annualize it for this sheet.

ITEM NEEDED	ANNUAL AMOUNT		MONTHLY AMOUNT
Real Estate Taxes	_____	/ 12 =	_____
Homeowners Insurance	_____	/ 12 =	_____
Home Repairs	_____	/ 12 =	_____
Replace Furniture	_____	/ 12 =	_____
Medical Bills	_____	/ 12 =	_____
Health Insurance	_____	/ 12 =	_____
Life Insurance	_____	/ 12 =	_____
Disability Insurance	_____	/ 12 =	_____
Car Insurance	_____	/ 12 =	_____
Car Repair/Tags	_____	/ 12 =	_____
Replace Car	_____	/ 12 =	_____
Clothing	_____	/ 12 =	_____
Tuition	_____	/ 12 =	_____
Bank Note	_____	/ 12 =	_____
IRS (Self-Employed)	_____	/ 12 =	_____
Vacation	_____	/ 12 =	_____
Gifts (incl. Christmas)	_____	/ 12 =	_____
Other _____	_____	/ 12 =	_____

RECOMMENDED PERCENTAGES

I have used a compilation of several sources and my own experience to derive the suggested percentage guidelines. However, these are only recommended percentages and will change dramatically if you have a very high or very low income. For instance, if you have a very low income, your necessities percentages will be high. If you have a high income, your necessities will be a lower percentage of income, and hopefully savings (not debt) will be higher than recommended.

ITEM	ACTUAL %	RECOMMENDED %
CHARITABLE GIFTS	_____	10–15%
SAVING	_____	5–10%
HOUSING		25–35%
UTILITIES	_____	5–10%
FOOD	_____	5–15%
TRANSPORTATION	_____	10–15%
CLOTHING	_____	2–7%
MEDICAL/HEALTH	_____	5–10%
PERSONAL	_____	5–10%
RECREATION	_____	5–10%
DEBTS	_____	5–10%

INSTRUCTIONS FOR
MONTHLY CASH-FLOW PLAN

Every dollar of your income should be allocated to some category on this sheet. Money "left over" should be put back into a category even if you have to make up a new category. You are making the spending decisions ahead of time here. Almost every category (except debt) should have some dollar amount in it. Example: If you do not plan ahead to replace the furniture, when you do replace it, it will cause strain or borrowing, so go ahead and plan now by saving. I have actually had people tell me that they can do without clothing. Oh, COME ON!! Be careful in your zeal to make the numbers work that you don't substitute the urgent for the important.

Fill in the amount for each subcategory under "Subtotal" and then the total for each main category under "Total." As you go through your first month, fill in the "Actually Spent" column with your real expenses or the saving you did for that area. If there is a substantial difference in the plan versus the reality, something has to give. You will either have to adjust the amount allocated to that area up and another down, or you will have to better control your spending in that area.

"% of Take-Home Pay" is the percentage of take-home pay that category represents; for example, what percentage of your total take-home pay did you spend on "Housing"? We will then compare your percentages with those on the "Recommended Percentages" sheet to determine if you need to consider adjusting your lifestyle.

An "*" beside an item means you should use the "envelope system."

The Emergency Fund should get ALL the savings until 3 to 6 months of expenses have been saved.

Note: Savings should be increased as you get closer to being debt free.

Hint: By saving early for Christmas and other gifts, you can get great buys and give better gifts for the same money.

- You have 3 "Monthly Cash-Flow Plan" sheets beginning on the next page.
- Use these forms as your "zero"-based budget forms, which should be checked every few weeks.
- Make enough copies to do this for a one-year period in order to help you develop proper financial management habits.

MONTHLY CASH-FLOW PLAN

Budgeted Item	Sub-total	TOTAL	Actually Spent	% of Take-Home Pay
CHARITABLE GIFTS		$300		10%
SAVING				
Emergency Fund	$50			
Retirement Fund				
College Fund		$50		
HOUSING				
First Mortgage	$725			
Second Mortgage				
Real Estate Taxes				
Homeowners Ins.				
Repairs or Mn. Fee				
Replace Furniture	$50			
Other _____		$775		
UTILITIES				
Electricity	$100			
Water	$50			
Gas	$50			
Phone	$50			
Trash				
Cable		$250		
***FOOD**				
*Grocery	$600			
*Restaurants	$100	$700		
TRANSPORTATION				
Car Payment				
Car Payment				
*Gas and Oil				
*Repairs and Tires				
Car Insurance				
License and Taxes				
Car Replacement				
PAGE 1 TOTAL		$2,075		

MONTHLY CASH-FLOW PLAN

Budgeted Item	Sub-total	TOTAL	Actually Spent	% of Take-Home Pay
CHARITABLE GIFTS		_____	_____	_____
SAVING				
Emergency Fund	_____		_____	
Retirement Fund	_____		_____	
College Fund	_____	_____	_____	_____
HOUSING				
First Mortgage	_____			
Second Mortgage	_____		_____	
Real Estate Taxes	_____		_____	
Homeowners Ins.	_____		_____	
Repairs or Mn. Fee	_____		_____	
Replace Furniture	_____		_____	
Other _____	_____	_____	_____	_____
UTILITIES				
Electricity	_____		_____	
Water	_____		_____	
Gas	_____		_____	
Phone	_____		_____	
Trash	_____		_____	
Cable	_____	_____	_____	_____
*FOOD				
*Grocery	_____		_____	
*Restaurants	_____	_____	_____	_____
TRANSPORTATION				
Car Payment	_____		_____	
Car Payment	_____		_____	
*Gas and Oil	_____		_____	
*Repairs and Tires	_____		_____	
Car Insurance	_____		_____	
License and Taxes	_____		_____	
Car Replacement	_____	_____	_____	_____
PAGE 1 TOTAL		_____	_____	

MONTHLY CASH-FLOW PLAN

Budgeted Item	Sub-total	TOTAL	Actually Spent	% of Take-Home Pay
*CLOTHING				
*Children	$100			
*Adults				
*Cleaning/Laundry		$100		
MEDICAL/HEALTH				
Disability Insurance	$100			
Health Insurance				
Doctor Bills	$50			
Dentist	$20			
Optometrist				
Drugs		$170		
PERSONAL				
Life Insurance	$50			
Child Care	$30			
*Baby-sitter				
*Toiletries				
*Cosmetics				
*Hair Care				
Education/Adult				
School Tuition				
School Supplies				
Child Support				
Alimony				
Subscriptions				
Organization Dues	$25			
Gifts (Incl. Christmas)				
Miscellaneous	$50			
*BLOW $$	$100	$255		
PAGE 2 TOTAL		$525		

MONTHLY CASH-FLOW PLAN

Budgeted Item	Sub-total	TOTAL	Actually Spent	% of Take-Home Pay
*CLOTHING				
*Children	_____		_____	
*Adults	_____		_____	
*Cleaning/Laundry	_____	_____	_____	_____
MEDICAL/HEALTH				
Disability Insurance	_____		_____	
Health Insurance	_____		_____	
Doctor Bills	_____		_____	
Dentist	_____		_____	
Optometrist	_____		_____	
Drugs	_____	_____	_____	_____
PERSONAL				
Life Insurance	_____		_____	
Child Care	_____		_____	
*Baby-sitter	_____		_____	
*Toiletries	_____		_____	
*Cosmetics	_____		_____	
*Hair Care	_____		_____	
Education/Adult	_____		_____	
School Tuition	_____		_____	
School Supplies	_____		_____	
Child Support	_____		_____	
Alimony	_____		_____	
Subscriptions	_____		_____	
Organization Dues	_____		_____	
Gifts (incl. Christmas)	_____		_____	
Miscellaneous	_____		_____	
*BLOW $$	_____	_____	_____	_____
PAGE 2 TOTAL		_____		

MONTHLY CASH-FLOW PLAN

Budgeted Item	Sub-total	TOTAL	Actually Spent	% of Take-Home Pay
RECREATION				
*Entertainment	$50		_____	
Vacation	$25	$75	_____	_____
DEBTS (Hopefully -0-)				
Visa 1	$100		_____	
Visa 2	_____		_____	
MasterCard 1	$75		_____	
MasterCard 2	_____		_____	
American Express	$50		_____	
Discover Card	_____		_____	
Gas Card 1	_____		_____	
Gas Card 2	_____		_____	
Dept. Store Card 1	_____		_____	
Dept. Store Card 2	_____		_____	
Finance Co. 1	_____		_____	
Finance Co. 2	_____		_____	
Credit Line	_____		_____	
Student Loan 1	$100		_____	
Student Loan 2	_____		_____	
Other _____	_____		_____	
Other _____	_____		_____	
Other _____	_____		_____	
Other _____	_____		_____	
Other _____	_____	$325	_____	_____
PAGE 3 TOTAL		$400	_____	
PAGE 2 TOTAL		$525	_____	
PAGE 1 TOTAL		$2075	_____	
GRAND TOTAL		$3000	_____	
TOTAL HOUSEHOLD **INCOME**		$3000		
		ZERO		

MONTHLY CASH-FLOW PLAN

Budgeted Item	Sub-total	TOTAL	Actually Spent	% of Take-Home Pay
RECREATION				
*Entertainment	_____		_____	
Vacation	_____	_____	_____	_____
DEBTS (Hopefully -0-)				
Visa 1	_____		_____	
Visa 2	_____		_____	
MasterCard 1	_____		_____	
MasterCard 2	_____		_____	
American Express	_____		_____	
Discover Card	_____		_____	
Gas Card 1	_____		_____	
Gas Card 2	_____		_____	
Dept. Store Card 1	_____		_____	
Dept. Store Card 2	_____		_____	
Finance Co. 1	_____		_____	
Finance Co. 2	_____		_____	
Credit Line	_____		_____	
Student Loan 1	_____		_____	
Student Loan 2	_____		_____	
Other _____	_____		_____	
Other _____	_____		_____	
Other _____	_____		_____	
Other _____	_____		_____	
Other _____	_____	_____	_____	_____
PAGE 3 TOTAL		_____	_____	
PAGE 2 TOTAL		_____	_____	
PAGE 1 TOTAL		_____	_____	
GRAND TOTAL		_____	_____	
TOTAL HOUSEHOLD INCOME		_____		
		ZERO		

- Put an asterisk beside every item that should be part of your "envelope system." The envelope system basically works like this: Put the amount in the monthly budget for a particular category in an envelope in CASH. Spend money out of that envelope for purchases in that category—and don't cheat by borrowing from other envelopes, or switch money from envelope to envelope through the month. The envelope system truly helps you control your spending in a particular category!

- Make enough copies of the Monthly Cash-Flow-plan to last a year.

Exercise #46

The Bigger Budget Picture

The vast majority of wage earners do not get an entire month's pay in one lump sum. Therefore, most people need a "cash-flow" plan. The following form assumes that you get paid once a week. If you get paid once every two weeks, just use fewer columns.
  Here are some basic rules:

1. Each column is a pay period. If you are a one-income household and you get paid two times a month, use two columns. If you both work and one is paid weekly and the other every two weeks, add the two paychecks together on the weeks you both get a paycheck.

2. Date the pay period columns, then enter the total income for that period. As you allocate your paycheck to an item, put the remaining total balance to the right of the slash. For example, if you plan to give $500 a month to charitable giving, you may be able to allocate only $100 of that from the first paycheck of the month, which leaves $400 to be allocated later. Some bills will "come out of each pay period" and some only from a selected pay period. For example, "Car Gas" may need to come out of every paycheck, but the electric bill may come from just one selected pay period.

3. Make sure you "spend" your entire paycheck before you get paid . . . ON PAPER. I don't care where you allocate your money, but allocate all of it before you get your check. No more management by crisis or impulse! Those who tend to be impulsive should just allocate more to the "Blow" category.

4. Many people have irregular incomes because they are self-employed or work on commission or royalties. Planning can be more difficult. Follow the instructions on the form provided for "Irregular-Income Planning."

5. Eventually, after your emergency fund is fully funded, you can start saving for certain items such as furniture, car replacement, home maintenance, or clothes. See the form labeled "Breakdown of Savings (p. 137)." This form will help remind you that ALL money is designated to SOMETHING. Keep up with your breakdown of monthly savings for one quarter at a time.

Key Concept #2

Make a Written Budget the "Boss" of Your Spending

Set up a new budget every month. Don't try to have the "perfect budget" for the "perfect month" because we never have either of those. Here are the basic rules related to your budget:

Simple Q & A

Q: According to American Express, a third of all consumers use _____ more frequently today than five years ago.

A: plastic

- If you are deep in the hole financially, there's a preliminary step you need to take. You MUST become current on your payments. If you are far behind, catch up on the necessities first—food, shelter, utilities, transportation, clothing. Only when you are current with the necessities can you begin to catch up on credit cards and student loans. (If you need more help at this level of financial crisis, see our Web site, daveramsey.com, or contact one of our personal trainers or certified counselors, or order the book *Financial Peace, Revisited.*)

- Spend every dollar *on paper* before the month begins. This is called a zero-based budget. Have somewhere for every dollar to go! Look at this month's income and this month's bills, savings, and debts, and match them up until you have given every income dollar an "outgo name."

- If you are married, agree on the budget with your spouse. It will be up to you to decide HOW you are going to come into agreement. I'm not a marriage counselor. But trust me on this: if you do NOT come into agreement, there's not much point in having the budget.

- Once you have the budget in place, the budget is the boss. If you need to make adjustments during the month, call an "emergency budget committee meeting." You may change the budget, and what you do with money, only if your spouse agrees to the change and the budget is still balanced at zero at the end of the month. For example, if you have an unexpected car repair that requires $50 you hadn't budgeted, you'll have to agree to spend $50 less in another category. The budget must balance out at zero. (You aren't the government, no negative numbers at the end of the month are allowed!)

INSTRUCTIONS FOR ALLOCATED-SPENDING PLAN

This sheet is where all your work thus far starts giving you some peace. You will implement your "Monthly Cash-Flow Plan" from theory into your life by using the "Allocated-Spending Plan." Note: If you have an irregular income, such as self-employment or commissions, you should use the "Irregular-Income Planning" sheet, after reviewing your Allocated-Spending Plan.

There are four columns to distribute as many as four different incomes within one month. Each column is one pay period. If you are a one-income household, and you get paid two times per month, then you will use only two columns. If both of you work, and one is paid weekly and the other every two weeks, add the two paychecks together on the weeks you both get a paycheck, while just listing the one paycheck on the other two. Date the pay-period columns, then enter the income for that period. As you allocate your paycheck to an item, put the remaining total balance to the right of the slash. Income for period 3/1 in our example is $1,000, and we are allocating $100 to Charitable Giving, leaving $900 to the right of the slash in that same column. Some bills will come out of each pay period and some only on selected pay periods. As an example, you may take "Car Gas" out of every paycheck, but pay the electric bill from period 2. You already pay some bills or payments out of designated checks, only now you pay all things from designated checks.

The whole point to this sheet, which is the culmination of all your monthly planning, is to allocate or "spend" your whole paycheck before you get paid. I don't care where you allocate your money, but allocate all of it before you get your check. Now all the tense, crisislike symptoms have been removed, because you planned. No more management by crisis or impulse. Those who tend to be impulsive should just allocate more to the "Blow" category. At least you are now doing it on purpose and not by default. The last blank that you make an entry in should have a "0" to the right of the slash, showing you have allocated your whole check.

An "*" beside an item means you should use the "envelope system."

Emergency Fund gets ALL the savings until 3 to 6 months of expenses have been saved.

SAMPLE ALLOCATED SPENDING PLAN

PAY PERIOD:	3/1			
ITEM				
INCOME	1,000			
CHARITABLE GIFTS	100/900	__/__	__/__	__/__
SAVING				
Emergency Fund(1)	50/850	__/__	__/__	__/__
Retirement Fund	__/__	__/__	__/__	__/__
College Fund	__/__	__/__	__/__	__/__
HOUSING				
First Mortgage	725/125	__/__	__/__	__/__

ALLOCATED-SPENDING PLAN

PAY PERIOD:	8/1	8/8	8/15	8/22
ITEM				
INCOME	$650	$850	$1,500	0
CHARITABLE GIFTS	75 /575	___/___	___/___	___/___
SAVING				
Emergency Fund	50 /525	___/___	___/___	___/___
Retirement Fund	___/___	___/___	___/___	___/___
College Fund	___/___	___/___	___/___	___/___
HOUSING				
First Mortgage	___/___	750 / 100	___/___	___/___
Second Mortgage	___/___	___/___	___/___	___/___
Real Estate Taxes	___/___	___/___	___/___	___/___
Homeowners Ins.	___/___	___/___	___/___	___/___
Repairs or Mn. Fees	___/___	___/___	___/___	___/___
Replace Furniture	50 / 475	___/___	___/___	___/___
Other _____	___/___	___/___	___/___	___/___
UTILITIES				
Electricity	100 /375	___/___	___/___	___/___
Water	50 / 325	___/___	___/___	___/___
Gas	___/___	50 / 50	___/___	___/___
Phone	___/___	25 / 25	___/___	___/___
Trash	___/___	___/___	___/___	___/___
Cable	___/___	25 / 0	___/___	___/___
*FOOD				
*Grocery	300 / 25	___/___	___/___	___/___
*Restaurants	25 / 0	___/___	___/___	___/___

ALLOCATED-SPENDING PLAN

PAY PERIOD: _____ _____ _____ _____

ITEM

INCOME _____ _____ _____ _____

CHARITABLE GIFTS ___/___ ___/___ ___/___ ___/___

SAVING

    Emergency Fund ___/___ ___/___ ___/___ ___/___

    Retirement Fund ___/___ ___/___ ___/___ ___/___

    College Fund ___/___ ___/___ ___/___ ___/___

HOUSING

    First Mortgage ___/___ ___/___ ___/___ ___/___

    Second Mortgage ___/___ ___/___ ___/___ ___/___

    Real Estate Taxes ___/___ ___/___ ___/___ ___/___

    Homeowners Ins. ___/___ ___/___ ___/___ ___/___

    Repairs or Mn. Fees ___/___ ___/___ ___/___ ___/___

    Replace Furniture ___/___ ___/___ ___/___ ___/___

    Other _____ ___/___ ___/___ ___/___ ___/___

UTILITIES

    Electricity ___/___ ___/___ ___/___ ___/___

    Water ___/___ ___/___ ___/___ ___/___

    Gas ___/___ ___/___ ___/___ ___/___

    Phone ___/___ ___/___ ___/___ ___/___

    Trash ___/___ ___/___ ___/___ ___/___

    Cable ___/___ ___/___ ___/___ ___/___

*FOOD

    *Grocery ___/___ ___/___ ___/___ ___/___

    *Restaurants ___/___ ___/___ ___/___ ___/___

ALLOCATED-SPENDING PLAN

TRANSPORTATION
    Car Payment   ____/____   ____/____   ____/____   ____/____
    Car Payment   ____/____   ____/____   ____/____   ____/____
    *Gas and Oil   ____/____   ____/____   ____/____   ____/____
    *Repairs and Tires   ____/____   ____/____   ____/____   ____/____
    Car Insurance   ____/____   ____/____   ____/____   ____/____
    License and Taxes   ____/____   ____/____   ____/____   ____/____
    Car Replacement   ____/____   ____/____   ____/____   ____/____
*CLOTHING
    *Children   ____/____   ____/____   ____/____   ____/____
    *Adults   ____/____   ____/____   ____/____   ____/____
    *Cleaning/Laundry   ____/____   ____/____   ____/____   ____/____
MEDICAL/HEALTH
    Disability Insurance   ____/____   ____/____   ____/____   ____/____
    Health Insurance   ____/____   ____/____   ____/____   ____/____
    Doctor   ____/____   ____/____   ____/____   ____/____
    Dentist   ____/____   ____/____   ____/____   ____/____
    Optometrist   ____/____   ____/____   ____/____   ____/____
    Drugs   ____/____   ____/____   ____/____   ____/____
PERSONAL
    Life Insurance   ____/____   ____/____   ____/____   ____/____
    Child Care   ____/____   ____/____   ____/____   ____/____
    *Baby-sitter   ____/____   ____/____   ____/____   ____/____
    *Toiletries   ____/____   ____/____   ____/____   ____/____
    *Cosmetics   ____/____   ____/____   ____/____   ____/____
    *Hair Care   ____/____   ____/____   ____/____   ____/____
    Education/Adult   ____/____   ____/____   ____/____   ____/____
    School Tuition   ____/____   ____/____   ____/____   ____/____
    School Supplies   ____/____   ____/____   ____/____   ____/____
    Child Support   ____/____   ____/____   ____/____   ____/____

ALLOCATED-SPENDING PLAN

Alimony	___/___	___/___	___/___	___/___
Subscriptions	___/___	___/___	___/___	___/___
Organization Dues	___/___	___/___	___/___	___/___
Gifts (incl. Christmas)	___/___	___/___	___/___	___/___
Miscellaneous	___/___	___/___	___/___	___/___
*BLOW $$	___/___	___/___	___/___	___/___
RECREATION				
*Entertainment	___/___	___/___	___/___	___/___
Vacation	___/___	___/___	___/___	___/___
DEBTS (Hopefully -0-)				
Visa 1	___/___	___/___	___/___	___/___
Visa 2	___/___	___/___	___/___	___/___
MasterCard 1	___/___	___/___	___/___	___/___
MasterCard 2	___/___	___/___	___/___	___/___
American Express	___/___	___/___	___/___	___/___
Discover Card	___/___	___/___	___/___	___/___
Gas Card 1	___/___	___/___	___/___	___/___
Gas Card 2	___/___	___/___	___/___	___/___
Dept. Store Card 1	___/___	___/___	___/___	___/___
Dept. Store Card 2	___/___	___/___	___/___	___/___
Finance Co. 1	___/___	___/___	___/___	___/___
Finance Co. 2	___/___	___/___	___/___	___/___
Credit Line	___/___	___/___	___/___	___/___
Student Loan 1	___/___	___/___	___/___	___/___
Student Loan 2	___/___	___/___	___/___	___/___
Other _____	___/___	___/___	___/___	___/___
Other _____	___/___	___/___	___/___	___/___
Other _____	___/___	___/___	___/___	___/___
Other _____	___/___	___/___	___/___	___/___
Other _____	___/___	___/___	___/___	___/___

IRREGULAR-INCOME PLANNING

Many of us have irregular incomes. If you are self-employed or work on commission or royalties, then planning your expenses is difficult, since you cannot always predict your income. You should still do all the sheets except the Allocated-Spending Plan. The Monthly Cash-Flow Plan will tell you what you have to earn monthly to survive or prosper, and those real numbers are very good for goal setting.

What you must do is take the items on the Monthly Cash-Flow Plan and prioritize them by importance. I repeat: by importance, not urgency. You should ask yourself, "If I only have enough money to pay one thing, what would that be?" Then ask, "If I only have enough money to pay one more thing, what would that be?" Move this way through the list. Now be prepared to stand your ground because things have a way of seeming important that are only urgent. Saving should be a high priority!

The third column, "Cumulative Amount," is the total of all amounts above that item. So, if you get a $2,000 check, you can see how far down your priority list you can go.

Item	Amount	Cumulative Amount
Penny's	$150	$150
Sears	$250	$400
Couch	$500	$900
Vacation - part	$200	$1,100
Christmas - part	$400	$1,500
Visa	$500	$2,000

IRREGULAR-INCOME PLANNING

Many of us have irregular incomes. If you are self-employed or work on commission or royalties, then planning your expenses is difficult, since you cannot always predict your income. You should still do all the sheets except the Allocated-Spending Plan. The Monthly Cash-Flow Plan will tell you what you have to earn monthly to survive or prosper, and those real numbers are very good for goal setting.

What you must do is take the items on the Monthly Cash-Flow Plan and prioritize them by importance. I repeat: by importance, not urgency. You should ask yourself, "If I only have enough money to pay one thing, what would that be?" Then ask, "If I only have enough money to pay one more thing, what would that be?" Move this way through the list. Now be prepared to stand your ground because things have a way of seeming important that are only urgent. Saving should be a high priority!

The third column, "Cumulative Amount," is the total of all amounts above that item. So, if you get a $2,000 check, you can see how far down your priority list you can go.

Item	Amount	Cumulative Amount
_____	_____	_____
_____	_____	_____
_____	_____	_____
_____	_____	_____
_____	_____	_____
_____	_____	_____
_____	_____	_____
_____	_____	_____

BREAKDOWN OF SAVINGS

After your emergency fund is fully funded, you can save for certain items like furniture, car replacement, home maintenance, or clothes, and your savings balance will grow. This sheet is designed to remind you that all of that money is committed to something, not just a Hawaiian vacation on impulse because you are now "rich." Keep up with your breakdown of savings monthly for one quarter at a time.

ITEM	BALANCE BY MONTH:	Sept.	Oct.	Nov.
Emergency Fund (1)	$1000			
Emergency Fund (2)	3-6 months			
Retirement Fund				
College Fund				
Real Estate Taxes				
Homeowners Insurance				
Repairs or Mn. Fee				
Replace Furniture		600	650	700
Car Insurance				
Car Replacement				
Disability Insurance				
Health Insurance				
Doctor				
Dentist		500	500	500
Optometrist				
Life Insurance				
School Tuition				
School Supplies				
Gifts (incl. Christmas)		600	700	800
Vacation		500	650	800
Other _____				
Other _____				
TOTAL		2200	2500	2800

BREAKDOWN OF SAVINGS

After your emergency fund is fully funded, you can save for certain items like furniture, car replacement, home maintenance, or clothes, and your savings balance will grow. This sheet is designed to remind you that all of that money is committed to something, not just a Hawaiian vacation on impulse because you are now "rich." Keep up with your breakdown of savings monthly for one quarter at a time.

ITEM	BALANCE BY MONTH:			
Emergency Fund (1)	$1000	_____	_____	_____
Emergency Fund (2)	3-6 months	_____	_____	_____
Retirement Fund		_____	_____	_____
College Fund		_____	_____	_____
Real Estate Taxes		_____	_____	_____
Homeowners Insurance		_____	_____	_____
Repairs or Mn. Fee		_____	_____	_____
Replace Furniture		_____	_____	_____
Car Insurance		_____	_____	_____
Car Replacement		_____	_____	_____
Disability Insurance		_____	_____	_____
Health Insurance		_____	_____	_____
Doctor		_____	_____	_____
Dentist		_____	_____	_____
Optometrist		_____	_____	_____
Life Insurance		_____	_____	_____
School Tuition		_____	_____	_____
School Supplies		_____	_____	_____
Gifts (incl. Christmas)		_____	_____	_____
Vacation		_____	_____	_____
Other _____		_____	_____	_____
Other _____		_____	_____	_____
TOTAL		_____	_____	_____

What About You?

Have you made your budget? Are you playing catch-up with past-due bills? Are you and your spouse in agreement about your budget? If not . . . stop now and make a budget. If you aren't caught up on "past-due" necessities (food, shelter, transportation, clothing), get caught up in these categories. If you and your spouse aren't in agreement, find a way to get to agreement!

NOTE: If you don't have a budget for this month, go back and make one! Do it now. Don't go forward until you have completed your budget!

Exercise #47

Quotes to Remember

Fill in the blanks! Use the Word Pool offered below if you need help.

1. You have to tell money what to do or it _____ .

2. "If you aim at nothing, you will hit it _____ time" (Zig Ziglar).

3. "Money is an excellent _____ and a horrible _____" (P. T. Barnum).

4. Money won't behave unless you _____ it.

5. "Which of you, intending to build a tower, does not sit down first and _____ the cost, whether he has enough to finish it" (Luke 14:28).

6. You can't build a House of Success without a _____ .

7. The power of _____ causes the Baby Steps to work.

8. You can get anywhere if you simply go _____ step at a time.

9. A budget needs to be _____—created new each month.

10. A study of Harvard graduates found that after two years, the 3 percent who had written goals achieved _____ financially than the other 97 percent combined.

11. Choose to be sick and tired of being _____ and _____.

12. There's no energy in logic. You have to get _____ (two-word phrase).

Word Pool

count • slave • one • leaves • priority • fired up • sick
written • tame • every • more • tired • blueprint • master

Answers:

1. leaves	4. tame	7. priority	10. more
2. every	5. count	8. one	11. sick; tired
3. slave; master	6. blueprint	9. written	12. fired up

Go back and read aloud these statements with the correct words filling the blanks!

Key Concept #3

Establish a Rainy-Day Fund

Baby Step One is: "Save $1,000 cash as a starter emergency fund." Why $1,000? That amount will cover the vast majority of "emergencies" faced by a family.

- If your family income is under $20,000 a year, start with an emergency fund of $500 and build up.

- If you spend any of the emergency fund, immediately go back to this baby step and replenish that fund.

Every person needs a rainy-day fund. Why? Because I can guarantee you this: It's going to RAIN!

What About You?

Think of a time in the last five years in which you WISH you had a rainy-day fund in place.

Exercise #48

The Value of an Umbrella

Money magazine says that 78 percent of us have a major negative event in any given ten-year period. Have you had such an event? Circle the number next to any item below that you or your family members have experienced in the last ten years.

1. Job loss because company was downsized, rightsized, or reorganized—or you were just plain fired
2. Divorce or legal separation
3. Unexpected pregnancy
4. Car blows up (or requires major repairs, such as transmission replaced)
5. Loved one dies
6. Grown kids move home again
7. Serious or prolonged illness, or hospitalization
8. Major dental bills
9. IRS audit results in tax bill

10. Accident or injury — personal or automobile

11. Natural catastrophe (such as damages from windstorm, tornado, hurricane, flood, forest fire)

12. Damage to home (such as broken pipes, fire, or ruptured sprinkler system)

13. Breakdown of major appliance (washing machine, dryer, television, water heater)

14. Theft or loss of valuable item that you use regularly (such as stolen briefcase, lost luggage, or travel damage to laptop computer)

15. Tire problems or damage to car (such as hailstorm dings)

16. Emergency surgery (such as appendectomy or hernia)

17. Child comes to live with you (owing to a family crisis, such as a death or disability of parent, resulting in child going to live with grandparents) on a full-time, summer-time, or part-time basis

18. Marriage

19. Crisis with elderly parent (requiring your financial assistance or provision)

20. Significant and upward adjustment in insurance premiums.

Still need convincing about the value of a rainy-day fund?

Exercise #49

Don't Touch It!

An emergency fund is for EMERGENCIES only. Determine if an item on the next page is a "true emergency" or "not an emergency":

True Emergency	Not an Emergency	
❏	❏	1. Not having set aside enough money for Christmas gift purchases
❏	❏	2. Vacation expenses
❏	❏	3. New tires and a lube job for the car
❏	❏	4. Back-to-school clothes and shoes
❏	❏	5. Checkups with dentist and physician
❏	❏	6. Summer camp for child
❏	❏	7. College tuition, lab fees, or books
❏	❏	8. Beautiful leather sofa on sale
❏	❏	9. Firewood for the fireplace
❏	❏	10. Cheerleading outfit or football uniform, or any other "gear" required by child who plays a sport, is part of a scouting group, or participates in extracurricular activities

Answer:

None of these are true emergencies. All should be planned for in a budget. Christmas comes the same time every year. They don't move it, so it should never sneak up on you!

You may be asking, "Why do you start with establishing an emergency fund when you are so opposed to DEBT?"

Because I've learned through the years that if people do not have this fund in place, they'll use just about any excuse to keep from sticking with a debt-reduction plan. If the alternator goes out on the car and they don't have an emergency fund, they'll put that $300 repair on a credit card and increase their debt. That one purchase can blow all their momentum in swearing off the use of credit cards or reducing credit-card debt.

Key Concept #4

Hide Your Emergency Money in an "Available" Location

If you keep your emergency money in an underwear drawer, you'll spend it on pizza delivery or impulse purchases. Hide your emergency funds in a bank savings account all its own. (Don't put it in your regular account or link the savings account to your checking account as an "overdraft protection" cushion.) The reason for the bank account is not to earn a good rate of return, but to make the money hard to get.

- Find a SAFE parking place for the money. A regular passbook savings account will suffice.

- You may want to be creative. A woman named Maria bought a cheap 8- by 10-inch frame and framed ten $100-bills in a stack. In the space within the frame, she wrote, "In case of emergency, break glass." She then hung the emergency fund on the wall behind coats in a closet. She figured the money was relatively safe there.

- Keep it in "liquid funds." This is not money to put in mutual funds, a retirement plan, or a certificate of deposit. Don't put it in a "fund" that has any kind of penalty for early withdrawal.

What About You?

Do you have your emergency fund in place? Is it in a safe, "liquid," accessible-but-not-readily-handy location?

If so, you're ready to take the next step . . .

7

Light Your Fire:
THE DEBT SNOWBALL

Total Money Makeover
Progress Check

Congratulations! You have taken the first step . . . and, as we all know, sometimes the first step is the most difficult, as well as the most important.

You have $1,000 in your "emergency fund." Feels good, doesn't it? (Did you think you couldn't do it? Now you know you CAN! That REALLY feels good, yes? ABSOLUTELY.)

This chapter is about Baby Step Two.

Key Concept #1
Take Hope That You Can Build
Genuine Wealth on Your Income

The most powerful wealth-building tool is your INCOME. Ideas, strategies, goals, vision, focus, and creative thinking all have their place, but it is when you get full control and use of your income that you build wealth—and not only build it, but keep it. A very small percentage of people may inherit money or win a jackpot, but these two avenues to wealth are the result of dumb luck. They are not a proven plan to financial fitness. To build wealth, you have to CONTROL your income.

The bottom line for becoming wealthy is this: Don't have any payments.

Debt is the enemy of your income. It keeps you from becoming wealthy. It keeps you from enjoying the feelings of security and flexibility associated with wealth.

One of the reasons I am so passionate about a person's getting rid of debt is because I've seen thousands of individuals make HUGE strides toward becoming millionaires in a relatively short time AFTER they get rid of their "payments."

Just think how much you could do with your income if you did NOT have a car payment, student loan, credit-card balance, medical debt, or even a mortgage.

What About You?

Have you ever thought about what it MIGHT be like if you didn't have ANY "required" expenses beyond this month's food, utility, fuel, and insurance payments? (Yes, eventually we can get rid of insurance payments, too!)

Case Study: Terry and Tina

When Terry and Tina began their Total Money Makeover they were a typical American couple. Married for five years and both twenty-seven years old, they had a combined $40,000 annual income. Their take-home pay was about $2,850 a month. They were just barely scraping by. (Tina worked only part-time while their four-year-old twin boys were in preschool.)

Terry and Tina had monthly payments of $850 for their house, $350 for one car, $180 for a second car, and a $165 student loan payment. They had credit-card debt of about $12,000, on which they were making monthly payments of $185. They also had purchased several items on "time payment" plans—furniture, a stereo system, and a personal loan. They spent $120 a month on these payments.

Terry and Tina had a total of $1,850 a month in fixed "payments."

If Terry and Tina had that amount to invest in a mutual fund, they would be millionaires in just fifteen years (by age forty-two). In the next five years, they could have $2 million. The numbers seem to grow exponentially from there:

At age fifty . . .	**$3 million**
At age fifty-two and a half . . .	**$4 million**
At age fifty-four and a half . . .	**$5 million**

Alas, Terry and Tina do NOT have $1,850 to invest every month. But they caught a vision for what it might be like if they did have that amount!

They set themselves on a tough path to achieving financial fitness and freedom. Within six years, they had paid off their regular monthly accounts AND their house! It helped that Terry got two raises during that period. Tina worked more hours when their twin sons entered school. They also made the choice to keep driving their old cars once they were paid for until the house was paid off.

Terry and Tina didn't fully start their investment plan until they turned thirty-four years old. Even so, they were looking at having their first million by the time they were in their late forties. They hoped to hit the $5-million mark by the time they turned sixty-two! And that wasn't counting on any salary raises or other increases they might receive in their income.

Exercise #50

Daydreaming About Your
Personal Financial Future

Take just a few minutes to do a little daydreaming about your future.

Revisit your current budget. Identify all things that are on a payment schedule of some type, and write down the month you have allocated for those payments on this month's budget:

PAYMENTS ON ACCOUNT:

Medical bills $_____

Credit-card payments $_____

Car payment(s) $_____

Student loans $_____

Other loans of any kind—any
account on which you are
making regular payments $_____

Subtotal: $_____

That's the amount you would have available to "INVEST FOR WEALTH" once you pay all these amounts in full.

HOUSE PAYMENT (minus the
part of your house payment
related to taxes and insurance) $_____

Total of house payment and
monthly payments on
outstanding accounts $_____

That's the amount you would have available to "INVEST FOR WEALTH" *every month* once you pay off all your outstanding balances and your home mortgage.

Multiply this number by 12: $_____

That's the amount you would have available EVERY YEAR to invest toward building true wealth. Fun to think about, isn't it?

Let's daydream further for just a moment that you invested only 75 percent of this in a wealth-building program. In other words, you set aside a quarter of this amount for pure fun and charitable giving.

Divide the last number above by 4: $_____

Now, what kind of fun could you have with that amount of money every year?

Identify three things you'd like to do with that sum:

1. _____

2. _____

3. _____

Hold those thoughts. You aren't there yet . . . but you can be someday!
End of fantasy. Now let's get back to the reality of making it happen.

Exercise #51

Going for the Goal!

Fill in the blanks below. Use the Word Pool provided if you need help. Really THINK about what you are writing and the statements you are completing!

1. The key to winning any battle is to _____ the enemy.

2. "Great spirits have always found violent opposition from _____ minds" (Albert Einstein).

3. Wealth building can be a reality—no longer just a dream—if you have no

   _____ .

4. The number one enemy of your income is _____ .

5. The path to financial freedom is simple to _____ but difficult to _____ (two-word phrase).

6. Taking control of your finances is 80 percent _____ and 20 percent head knowledge.

7. Focus the sun's rays through a magnifying glass, and you can start a _____. Focus your energies on paying off one bill at a time, smallest to largest, and you can light a fire under your desire to become debt-free!

8. Focused intensity declares, "To the _____ of virtually everything else, I'm getting out of debt!"

9. "My son, if you become surety for your friend, . . . _____ yourself like a gazelle from the hand of the hunter, and like a bird from the hand of the fowler" (Prov. 6:1, 5).

10. The way out of debt is to outmaneuver the enemy and _____ for your life!

Word Pool

debt • understand • deliver • mediocre • exclusion
walk out • run • fire • identify • behavior • payments

Answers:

1. identify
2. mediocre
3. payments
4. debt
5. understand; walk out

6. behavior
7. fire
8. exclusion
9. deliver
10. run

Go back and read aloud each of these statements with the correct words filling the blanks!

Key Concept #2

Start the Debt Snowball

The Debt Snowball is the key to paying off your debts. Forms are found on the following pages. The process is EASY to understand, but it can require truckloads of effort. Here are the basics to get the snowball rolling downhill:

- List all your debts except your house payment. Include loans from Mom and Dad, medical debts that have zero interest, ALL debts!

- Now, relist those debts in order from smallest to largest. Put the smallest debt at the top of the list, the largest at the bottom. (The only time to pay off a larger debt first is if it is related to a big-time emergency, such as owing the IRS and having them come after you with a threat to take away your house.)

- Make a focused and diligent effort to pay off the smallest debt (the one at the top of your list). Make minimum payments to stay current on all the other accounts, but put every other available dollar in your budget toward paying off the smallest debt.

- Once you have paid off the smallest debt, take on the next debt. Take the amount that is now "freed up" from paying the smallest debt and apply it toward the next debt. Add any other money you can "find" in your budget that month to pay on the next smallest debt. (Once you get this going, you tend to "find" more money you can apply!) When the number two bill is paid off, take on the number three bill, and so forth, until all the bills are paid. Keep paying minimums on all the debts except the one you are concentrating on.

- Develop an "ATTACK!" mentality. Every time the Snowball rolls over and down to another debt, it picks up more snow and gets larger until eventually . . . you have an avalanche!

Many people get to the bottom of the credit-card and minor-payments list and find they have more than $1,000 they can apply to paying off a car loan or student loan. Once those are out of the way, it doesn't take long to be debt-free except for a house mortgage!

Case Study: The "Fridge" Lady

One woman we call the "Fridge Lady" took her Debt Snowball form to the local copy shop and had it enlarged to supersize. Then she put it on her refrigerator door. Every time she paid off a debt, she drew a big red line through it on her list. She told me that each time she walked through the kitchen and looked at that refrigerator door, she would yell, "Oh, yeah, we are getting out of debt!"

If that sounds corny to you, perhaps you'd like to know that this woman has a Ph.D. She is not a low-class or dumb person. She is so sophisticated and intelligent that she understood the underlying principle for the Debt Snowball—motivating yourself to turn your spending behavior into paying-off-debt behavior. She understood the power of small but quick wins in motivating a person to change behavior.

Exercise #52

The Debt Snowball

On the following pages is the Debt Snowball form (and there's also a completed sample to help you get started).

- List your debts in descending order with the smallest payoff or balance first.

- Do not be concerned with interest rates or terms unless two debts have similar payoffs, then list the higher-interest-rate debt first.

- Paying off the little debts first shows you quick progress and motivates you to stick with the plan.

- Duplicate the blank sheet and redo it each time you pay off a debt so you can see how close you are getting to financial freedom! Keep the old sheets to wallpaper the bathroom in your new debt-free house!

- Each month the new "Payment" total is found by adding all the payments on the debts listed ABOVE that item to the payment you are working on.

- "Payments Remaining" is the number of payments remaining when you get down to the snowball effect for that item.

- "Cumulative Payments" is the total payment needed, including the snowball, to pay off the item. It is your running total for all payments remaining.

THE DEBT SNOWBALL

List your debts in order with the smallest payoff or balance first. Do not be concerned with interest rates or terms unless two debts have similar payoffs, then list the higher-interest-rate debt first. Paying the little debts off first gives you quick feedback, and you are more likely to stay with the plan.

   Redo this sheet each time you pay off a debt, so you can see how close you are getting to freedom. Keep the old sheets to wallpaper the bathroom in your new debt-free house. The "New Payment" is found by adding all the payments on the debts listed above that item to the payment you are working on, so you have compounding payments, which will get you out of debt very quickly. "Payments Remaining" is the number of payments remaining on that debt when you get down the snowball to that item. "Cumulative Payments" is the total payments needed, including the snowball, to pay off that item. In other words, this is your running total for "Payments Remaining."

COUNTDOWN TO FREEDOM!!

Date:_____

Item	Total Payoff	Minimum Payment	New Payment	Payments Remaining	Cumulative Payments
Penny's	*$150*	*$15*	*$0*	*0*	*Garage sale*
Sears	*$250*	*$10*	*$25*	*11*	*11*
Visa	*$500*	*$75*	*$100*	*Pd.*	*11*
M.C.	*$1,500*	*$90*	*$190*	*5*	*16*
Car	*$4,000*	*$210*	*$400*	*4*	*20*
Stu. Loan	*$4,000*	*$65*	*$465*	*6*	*26*

TOTALLY debt free except the house!

Finish Emergency Fund
Fund Retirement/College
Then Pay Off House

THE DEBT SNOWBALL

List your debts in order with the smallest payoff or balance first. Do not be concerned with interest rates or terms unless two debts have similar payoffs, then list the higher-interest-rate debt first. Paying the little debts off first gives you quick feedback, and you are more likely to stay with the plan.

   Redo this sheet each time you pay off a debt, so you can see how close you are getting to freedom. Keep the old sheets to wallpaper the bathroom in your new debt-free house. The "New Payment" is found by adding all the payments on the debts listed above that item to the payment you are working on, so you have compounding payments, which will get you out of debt very quickly. "Payments Remaining" is the number of payments remaining on that debt when you get down the snowball to that item. "Cumulative Payments" is the total payments needed, including the snowball, to pay off that item. In other words, this is your running total for "Payments Remaining."

COUNTDOWN TO FREEDOM!!

Date:_____

Item	Total Payoff	Minimum Payment	New Payment	Payments Remaining	Cumulative Payments

Key Concept #3

Stop Borrowing

As you start the Debt Snowball, you must take a simultaneous step: Stop borrowing. Otherwise, you will just be changing the names of the creditors on your list of debts. Draw a line in the sand and say, "I will never borrow again."

Now, as soon as you make this statement, you are likely to have a serious temptation to engage in impulse shopping. Or an emergency will hit. Nevertheless, you have to stop borrowing—as in, stop buying on credit cards—or you won't succeed.

You need a PLASTECTOMY . . . that's plastic surgery on your credit cards. In other words, you need to cut up your credit cards!

Don't think about it—just do it. Have fun cutting away what have been shackles on your ability to achieve financial fitness and freedom, and even on your peace of mind.

Exercise #53

The Cutting Party

Lay your credit cards in a stack on a table before you. Grab a big pair of scissors—and start whacking away at the cards. As you cut up each card, say aloud, "No more. I'm on my way to financial fitness and freedom!"

Simple Q & A

Q: According to the *Wall Street Journal,* nearly _____ percent of all consumers live from paycheck to paycheck.

A: 70

Key Concept #4

*Adopt the Mind-Set and
INTENSITY of a Gazelle*

In an earlier exercise, I quoted Proverbs 6:5, which says, "Deliver yourself like a gazelle from the hand of the hunter, and like a bird from the hand of the fowler."

The first time I really read this verse in a daily Bible study, I thought the gazelle was a cute little animal metaphor. Then one day later that week, I was surfing channels and hit the Discovery Channel. They were filming gazelles. The gazelles were peacefully grazing when suddenly a cheetah came sneaking through the bushes looking for lunch. One of the gazelles caught a whiff of Mr. Cheetah and spread the alert, "Cheetah nearby!" Not able to see the cheetah they were smelling, the gazelles stood in something of a frozen position lest they run right toward Mr. Cheetah. Mr. Cheetah made his move and leaped from the bushes. The gazelles all yelled, "CHEETAH!" and took off running. (Actually they didn't yell, but they did run like crazy in fourteen different directions.)

At this point, the Discovery Channel informed us that the cheetah is the fastest mammal on dry land. He can go from zero to forty-five miles an hour in four leaps. There's no way a gazelle can outrun a cheetah.

Ah, but a gazelle can *outmaneuver* a cheetah. The gazelles don't run from a cheetah in a straight line. They continually change directions, which tires out the cheetah. The result is, the lightning-quick cheetah only has a gazelle burger for lunch in one out of nineteen chases! The gazelle wins almost every time.

What does this mean to you as a person focused on getting out of debt?

Two things: First, you need to outmaneuver every temptation that is going to come at you to spend. Don't even glance at those get-rich-quick schemes, intellectual theories, or new-credit-card-reserved-in-your-name messages that are sure to come your way.

Second, perhaps you need to perform a drastic jump-start on the Debt Snowball. This is especially important if you have such a mountain of monthly payments that you can't seem to find ANY extra money to apply to a quick payoff of your smallest debt.

Jump-Starting the Debt Snowball

One of the most dynamite-style ways of jump-starting the Debt Snowball is to SELL SOMETHING. You might clean out the attic or the garage and sell lots of little stuff at a garage sale . . . or perhaps sell a seldom-used item on the Internet . . . or sell a big, precious item through the classified ads. I've seen people sell everything from goldfish from a pond to a Harley motorcycle to a knife collection to a sailboat. I've seen people sell things from nonfamily antiques to automobiles.

My rule of thumb for selling or keeping items is this: Apart from your home, if you can't get debt-free on it in eighteen to twenty months, sell it. That goes for cars and boats, too.

My great-grandfather ran a timber operation in the hills of Kentucky and West Virginia. In that era, the timber cutters put logs in the river to float them downstream to the sawmill. At times, the logs might build up at a bend in the river and create a traffic jam of wood. Sometimes the loggers could break up these jams by pushing the logs. At other times, if the logjam was especially tight, they might have to throw a stick of dynamite into the water.

Selling items to pay off debt is a little bit like dynamite. It can seem like a drastic step at the time. It makes for a good story later. But overall, it accomplishes the goal—it gets the Debt Snowball rolling!

Other Possible Solutions or "Add-On" Efforts

There are a few other things you can do to get the Debt Snowball moving:

- Volunteer to work "overtime" or "more hours."

- Get a second part-time job.

- Cut back on "frill" or "luxury" items—for example, stop getting the daily paper (you can read it at a library on your lunch hour), stop paying for cable television or a satellite dish, stop paying for a second phone line, stop paying for a cell phone. You may think you can't live without these items. The truth is, cable TV and cellular phones were virtually nonexistent forty years ago, and people got along just fine! Just cutting out the four items I listed above can save you more than $100 a month. That's significant.

Exercise #54

What Could You Sell?

You may not need to sell anything to get the Debt Snowball rolling downhill, but think about what you COULD sell if you needed to "earn" a few hundred dollars in the next sixty days from the SALE of items currently in your possession. Below, list ten things you could sell fairly quickly in a garage sale or through local advertising. Choose items you aren't using or no longer see a need to keep.

1. _____
2. _____
3. _____
4. _____
5. _____
6. _____
7. _____
8. _____
9. _____
10. _____

Are you are still making payments on any of the items listed in the exercise on the previous page? If so . . . make sure you could sell those items for MORE than you still owe. Put a star by these items. They are items that give you a "double benefit"—you no longer have the payments on those items (which means they may come off your debt list), AND you will have a little income from the item to apply to other debt.

For example, one woman bought a treadmill thinking she would walk her way to fitness in the privacy of her own home. She rarely used the treadmill and found that she actually enjoyed walking more if she walked in her neighborhood with a friend. She had purchased the treadmill for $2,300 and was making a $100 payment on it each month. She still had $1,400 to pay on the treadmill. She advertised the item for $1,795 in the classified ads section of her community newspaper—she identified it as a "bargain price" on a virtually unused item that had retailed for $2,295. She eventually sold the treadmill for $1,700. This woman got the "double benefit"—she eliminated a $100 a month payment from her debt list, and she had $300 left over to apply to her next smallest bills. Actually, that amount more than paid for her $122 cellular phone and a $129 outstanding medical bill. She wiped three bills off her debt list with one sale (including the treadmill payment) and made a good dent in a fourth bill!

Key Concept #5

Be Smart About Second Mortgages, Business Debt, and Rental Property Mortgages

Some people ask where they should "put" items such as second mortgages, business debts, and rental property mortgages. Here are my simple rules:

1. If a second mortgage is MORE than 50 percent of your gross annual income, do not put it in the Debt Snowball. Put it with

your home mortgage and deal with it later. But if the amount is LESS than 50 percent of your gross annual income, put it in the Debt Snowball. For example, if you make $40,000 a year, and the second mortgage is $15,000, put it in the Debt Snowball; if it is $25,000, put it with your first mortgage. DO consider, however, refinancing your first and second mortgages together if you can lower both interest rates.

2. Most small-business owners have some debt, and most of this debt is personally guaranteed, which means it is really personal debt. Treat small-business debt like any other debt. If, however, your business debt is LARGER than half your gross annual income or half your home mortgage, hold the payoff on that debt until later.

3. Hold any rental-property mortgages until later . . . but don't buy any more rental property now.

Overall, the Debt Snowball is for relatively small and medium-sized debts.

Weigh Your Options

There are some "trade-off" situations you should seriously consider. For example, if you own rental property that has $40,000 in equity, and you also have $40,000 in credit-card debt, sell that piece of property and pay off your credit cards. It's highly unlikely you are earning more from your rentals than you are paying in interest on your cards.

If you have several pieces of rental property, consider selling one or more and paying off the rest of the property in full.

You may want to cut out some things that are COSTING you money and time, to free up time you can spend in a second "temporary" job. For example, one woman was spending an hour a day working out at a health club, plus spending $50 a month for the privilege of doing so. She got a part-time JOB at the health club (working three evenings a week at hours other employees didn't want to work). She was allowed to use the equipment and other facilities for free as an employee. She not only dropped the $50 club-membership payment from her budget, but she ADDED net income of about $70 a week to her budget.

What About You?

Get creative. What might YOU do to increase your income or reduce your outgo each month? What might YOU do to handle your assets more wisely?

Bonus Concept:
Talk to Your Creditors

You may need to work out a payment plan with your creditors. On the next couple of pages you'll find forms that will help you take a look at your debts and then develop a plan. You'll also find two letters to use as examples for writing your creditors.

If you cannot pay your creditors what they request, you should treat them all fairly and the same. You should pay even the ones who are not jerks, and pay everyone as much as you can. Many creditors will accept a written plan and cut special deals with you as long as you are communicating, maybe even overcommunicating, and sending them something. We have had clients use this even when sending only $2 payments and survive for literally years.

Pro Rata means "their share": the percent of total debt each creditor represents. That will determine how much you send them. Then, you send the check with a budget and this sheet attached each month, even if the creditor says they will not accept it.

PRO RATA DEBTS

Discover	$1,200	$150
Citibank Visa	300	45
MBNA Visa	200	25
Penny's	100	60
Sears	200	30
TOTAL	$2,000	$310

Income	$2,400
-Necessity Expense	2,200
Disposable Income	$ 200

Can't Increase Income Anytime Soon

PRO RATA PLAN

Item	Total Payoff	/Debt	= Percent	Disposable X Income	= New Payments
Discover	1,200	/ 2000	= . 60	X 200	= 120
Citibank	300	/ 2000	= . 15	X 200	= 30
MBNA	200	/ 2000	= . 10	X 200	= 20
Penny's	100	/ 2000	= . 5	X 200	= 10
Sears	200	/ 2000	= . 10	X 200	= 20

PRO RATA DEBTS

Item	Total Payoff	Total /Debt	=Percent	Disposable X Income	New = Payments
_____	_____	/_____	=.____	X_____	=_____
_____	_____	/_____	=.____	X_____	=_____
_____	_____	/_____	=.____	X_____	=_____
_____	_____	/_____	=.____	X_____	=_____
_____	_____	/_____	=.____	X_____	=_____
_____	_____	/_____	=.____	X_____	=_____
_____	_____	/_____	=.____	X_____	=_____
_____	_____	/_____	=.____	X_____	=_____
_____	_____	/_____	=.____	X_____	=_____
_____	_____	/_____	=.____	X_____	=_____
_____	_____	/_____	=.____	X_____	=_____
_____	_____	/_____	=.____	X_____	=_____
_____	_____	/_____	=.____	X_____	=_____
_____	_____	/_____	=.____	X_____	=_____
_____	_____	/_____	=.____	X_____	=_____
_____	_____	/_____	=.____	X_____	=_____
_____	_____	/_____	=.____	X_____	=_____
_____	_____	/_____	=.____	X_____	=_____
_____	_____	/_____	=.____	X_____	=_____
_____	_____	/_____	=.____	X_____	=_____
_____	_____	/_____	=.____	X_____	=_____
_____	_____	/_____	=.____	X_____	=_____
_____	_____	/_____	=.____	X_____	=_____

PRO RATA PLAN LETTER

Date: Feb. 22, 2002

From: Joe and Suzie Public
123 Anystreet
Anytown, ST 11111

To: Mega Credit Card Company
999 Main Street
Big City, ST 00000

Re: Joe and Suzie Public # 1234-5678-9012-9999

Dear Collection Manager:

Recently I lost my job, and my wife is employed in a clerical position. We have met with a financial counselor to assess our present situation.

We acknowledge our indebtedness to you of $6000, and fully intend to pay you back in full. However you are one of 6 creditors that we owe a total of $42,968 to. We owe minimum payments of $782 each month. We are not able to meet these minimum payments at the present time, and we are not planning on going into further debt to meet these obligations.

We have put together a basic necessities cash-flow plan based on our take-home pay of $2340 per month (see the enclosed copy of cash-flow plan). Since we have 2 small children and no disposable income at this time to pay our creditors, we cannot make a payment to you at the present time, but we do not intend to go bankrupt.

At this time we are asking for a moratorium on payments for the next 120 days. We will keep in close contact with you and, as soon as possible, we will begin making payments. If possible, we would like to request a reduction on interest during this time.

We are aware that this is an inconvenience to you, but we must meet the basic needs of our family first. We fully intend to pay our creditors all that we owe them. Please be patient with us. If you have any questions please contact us at 600-555-9876.

Thank you for your consideration of our present situation.

Sincerely,

Joe Public
Suzie Public
Joe and Suzie Public

PRO RATA PLAN LETTER

Date: _____

From: _____

_____

_____

To: Name of Creditor
Address

Re: Cardholder name and account number

Dear: *(If you know a specific person or, when contacting them by phone, get name of area or office supervisor.)*

Recently (I have had to........................... [or] my husband had......................) change jobs and have met with a financial counselor to access our present situation.

We acknowledge our indebtedness to you of $_____, and fully intend to pay you back in full. However you are one of _____ creditors that we owe a total of $ _____ to. We owe minimum payments of $ _____ each month. We are not able to meet these minimum payments at the present time, and we are not planning on going into further debt to meet these obligations.

We have put together a basic necessities cash-flow plan based on our take-home pay of $_____ per month (enclose copy of cash-flow plan). Since we have _____ small children and no (or limited) disposable income at this time to pay our creditors, we (can or cannot) make a payment to you (of $_____) at the present time, but we do not intend to go bankrupt.

At this time we are asking for a moratorium on payments for the next _____ (30, 60, 90, or 120) days. We will keep in close contact with you and, as soon as possible, we will begin making payments. If possible, we would like to request a reduction on interest during this time.

We are aware that this is an inconvenience to you, but we must meet the basic needs of our family first. We fully intend to pay our creditors all that we owe them. Please be patient with us. If you have any questions please contact us at _____ (phone number).

Thank you for your consideration of our present situation.

Sincerely,

(Signatures)

$$8$$

Kick Murphy Out:
A FULL EMERGENCY FUND

Total Money Makeover
Progress Check

Okay . . . breathe deeply. It generally takes people eighteen to twenty months to complete the first two steps in the Total Money Makeover plan. By the time you reach this step:

- You have $1,000 in cash, and

- you have no debt except your home mortgage.

You have pushed with intensity. Momentum is on your side. Pause for a moment to anticipate what it will feel like when you are debt-free except for your house and you have $1,000 set aside in a rainy-day fund. Do I see you smiling?

This chapter is about Baby Step Three.

Key Concept #1
Finish Your Emergency Fund

This step can usually happen quickly because you no longer have any payments. The step is this: Finish your emergency fund so you have a full three to six months of expenses in it. In essence, you are "upping" your initial emergency fund of $1,000 to a range that's usually from $5,000 to $25,000. A typical family making $3,000 a month might have a $10,000 emergency fund as a minimum.

If I saw you smiling at having $1,000 set aside, how big are you smiling at having $10,000 in savings?

Why three to six months' worth of income? That's what Financial Planners and Financial Counselors through the years have established as a general rule of thumb. It easily can take a person three months to find a new job after a job loss or to recover from a serious accident.

I strongly recommend SIX MONTHS for those who are:

- Self-employed

- Working on a straight commission basis

- Single or have a one-income married household

- Having chronic medical problems in the family

- Working in an unstable job situation

If you are in a steady, "secure" job that you've had for fifteen years, and everyone in your family is healthy, you may opt for the THREE-MONTH figure.

Parenting magazine has reported that 49 percent of Americans stated in a survey they could cover LESS THAN ONE MONTH'S EXPENSES if they suddenly lost their income. In other words, half the families of our nation have virtually no buffer against emergencies. You've heard of Murphy—the one with all the laws related to catastrophes? If you have no buffer against emergencies, you may as well invite Murphy to move in and take up permanent residence.

Don't Use This Money Unless
It Is ABSOLUTELY Necessary

Your emergency fund is NOT something you should dip into without careful thought and prayer. Even if you feel as if something is an emergency, give yourself a little "cooling-off" period before you rush to pull money out of this fund. You may be able to handle the emergency by readjusting your budget.

At the same time, if you see an emergency on the horizon, you may be smart to turn from Debt Snowballing to building up an emergency fund. For example, if you are expecting a baby in three months and you know your husband's manufacturing plant is closing in four months, you'll probably want to have emergency funds in place!

Keep the Fund "Liquid"

You need to keep your emergency fund in "liquid" form—generally a money-market fund or another type of fund that doesn't have a penalty associated with early withdrawal. I like a money-market account with no penalties and full check-writing privileges. We have a large emergency fund for our household in a mutual fund company money-market account. Some money-market accounts such as these pay as much interest as a one-year CD. (Some CDs now have a "quick-release" feature that allows one withdrawal during the committed period without penalty.)

Do NOT put this emergency-fund money in savings bonds, bonds, or other "low-risk" investments. The point is not to earn a return on this money, but to have this money available to protect you in life's storms, to give you peace of mind, and to keep your focus on staying out of debt.

The Less-"Secure" Spouse Wins

If you are married, you need to set the actual amount of your emergency fund with your spouse. Very often one spouse feels a need to have more money in this fund than the other. That person wins.

I encourage you to recognize that the sexes tend to view emergency funds differently. In general, men are more task- and action-oriented and they want their money out there, working for them. They are more willing to take risks. Women are more security-oriented. They tend to like the fact that they have $10,000 in a rainy-day fund, even if it's only drawing minimal interest.

What Is an Emergency?

It is useful to think about what might constitute an emergency. Read through the two lists below to get a little clearer picture about what is truly an EMERGENCY:

A True Emergency	Something You Should Have Anticipated and Budgeted
Paying the deductible on medical, homeowners, or car insurance after an accident	Fixing up the boat (unless you live on it)
Medical bills (your part after an accident or unforeseen illness)	Prom dress or tuxedo rental
	Starting your own business
Blown engine on the car you need to use to get to work	Trip to Cancún
	Big sale at your favorite department store
Removal of an uprooted tree from your driveway after a storm	College tuition

What About You?

How secure do you feel about your ability to handle life financially if you lost your job and knew you had no income for the next three months? What is the actual dollar amount that you calculate you would have in an emergency fund to provide adequate income to meet your expenses for that period?

Exercise #55

Your Emergency Fund

What is your total GROSS income at present PER MONTH:

$ _____ per month

Multiply this number by 3: _____ This is the MINIMUM you should have in a fully established rainy-day emergency fund.

Multiply the gross-income number above by 6: _____ This is the MAXIMUM you should have in a fully established rainy-day emergency fund.

GOAL: The range you want as a goal for your fully established rainy-day emergency fund is: $ _____ to $ _____ .

Case Study: Dave and Sharon

I have already told you that Sharon and I were millionaires and then lost everything when we were still in our twenties. As two people who crashed and were at the bottom, you can imagine that the subject of an "emergency fund" is a critical one in my home.

I readily admit that our financial crash was totally my doing: It was a real-estate business screwup that Sharon watched before she took the downhill ride with me. One of the wounds in our relationship is this issue of security. It doesn't take much for Sharon's emotions to "re-feel" the fear of looking into the faces of a brand-new baby and a toddler and not knowing how we were going to keep the heat on. I am aware of this sensitive place in her psyche; I know it's there for good reason.

Therefore . . . we don't use our emergency fund even for emergencies. Part of the salve I needed to put on this wound in our relationship is an "emergency fund" for our emergency fund! Being the highly trained investment mogul that I am, I could certainly find places to put our emergency-fund money where it could earn more. Or would it? Remember, personal finance is PERSONAL. I have come to realize that if I even walk near the drawer where the emergency fund money-market checkbook is kept, Sharon's security gland can tighten up. I know she has peace of mind only with an oversized emergency fund. That peace of mind IS what this oversized fund EARNS.

Guys, take it from me. A generous emergency fund can be a wonderful gift to your wife, and it can add strength to your marriage.

Exercise #56

*The Advantages of Your
Emergency Fund*

Fill in the blanks of the sentences below. Use the Word Pool provided if you need to.

1. An emergency fund can turn a crisis into an _____.

2. An emergency fund can keep you focused on reducing _____ rather than increasing debt.

3. An emergency-fund dollar amount should be set by the person who has the greatest need for financial _____ .

4. As you change your money habits, you will likely find that you use an emergency fund less and _____ .

5. As you change your money habits, you may find that you change your idea about what truly constitutes an _____ .

6. Once an emergency fund is in place, you may find that what used to be huge, life-altering events become simply _____ challenges.

7. Even if your income is _____ (such as receiving money from a pension plan), you need an emergency fund.

8. One of the best things about living your life on principle is that a very high percentage of your _____ are already made.

Word Pool

debt • security • emergency • inconvenience
budget • less • guaranteed • decisions

Answers:

1. inconvenience

2. debt

3. security

4. less

5. emergency

6. budget

7. guaranteed

8. decisions

Go back and read aloud each of these statements with the correct words filling the blanks!

Simple Q & A

Q: Credit cards are big business for the lenders. Capitol One and MBNA, two of the major issuers of credit cards, spend $ _____ each QUARTER on credit-card offers, according to CardWeb, Inc.

A: $60 to $70 MILLION

Bonus Concept:
Delay the Purchase of a Home

I am a strong advocate of home ownership, and I love real estate as an investment. I believe in both the financial and emotional advantages of home ownership. But . . . if you are in debt and you don't own a house yet, I encourage you to delay saving for a house down payment until AFTER you have cleared away your debts and you have a fully funded rainy-day emergency fund in place. I have seen too many stressed-out young couples rush into buying something before they were either financially or emotionally ready to take on the responsibilities related to home ownership.

If you don't have a house mortgage, and you DO have a $1,000 emergency fund, no debts, and three to six months' worth of income in liquid investments, you are in a GREAT position to start serious wealth building.

Be Financially Healthy for Life:
MAXIMIZE RETIREMENT INVESTING

Total Money Makeover
Progress Check

At this point:

- You are debt-free except your house, and
- you have three to six months of expenses (usually about $10,000 minimum) in an emergency fund.

You are poised to start building wealth!
This chapter covers Baby Step Four.

Key Concept #1

Decide How You Want to
Live in Your Retirement Years

Investing for retirement in a Total Money Makeover doesn't necessarily mean investing to quit your job. Too often, retirement in America has come to mean "save enough money so I can quit the job I hate." That's a bad life plan. If you hate your career path, change it.

Retirement in a Total Money Makeover is defined in terms of SECURITY. Security allows a person to make choices—work may be one of those choices. A person may want to write a book, take up art lessons, play eighteen holes of golf a day, spend more time with grandkids, or study something he's always wanted to study.

Retirement in a Total Money Makeover also includes the concept of FINANCIAL DIGNITY. This happens only with a plan.

Let's review where you are by the time you reach this stage in your Total Money Makeover. You have attacked your debt, and it is gone. With the extra money you had in your budget after eliminating your debt, you attacked the goal of building an emergency fund with three to six months of income in it, and you have that funded by now. You are at a crucial time. The only thing you have left to pay off is your house. What you do with the extra money that you poured into the emergency fund and debt payoff is now yours to INVEST.

Before you can decide how to invest, you need to come to terms with how you want to LIVE in your "golden years."

What About You?

How do you define *retirement*? What hopes do you have for the "golden years" of your life?

Exercise #57

Dreaming of Retirement

On the next page, write down ten activities or experiences—both ongoing and one-time experiences—you dream about having in your "retirement years." If you don't plan ever to retire from your career or from working at a job you love, write down "CONTINUE WORKING!" on the first line.

1. _____
2. _____
3. _____
4. _____
5. _____
6. _____
7. _____
8. _____
9. _____
10. _____

Now go back and prioritize the top four of these goals. (You may just want to put a star by them instead of numbering them 1–4.)

Ask yourself: Are these ten activities or experiences what I truly DREAM of doing, or just what I think I WILL be doing? Make adjustments so you have down your DREAM activities and experiences. Describe your ideal retirement.

Now relist these ten activities and experiences in the blanks below, and in the space to the right of each item, identify the plan that you already have in place for transitioning into that activity. For example, if your dream is to travel to Tahiti and spend six months there, write down what can you start doing NOW to prepare for that—identify things from researching travel brochures and condo-sharing programs to making a budget for the excursion to setting aside funds earmarked for the excursion. If your dream is to spend time teaching your grandson to fish, you might need to have a plan that includes moving closer to your grandson, identifying a series of fishing holes you hope to visit together, or making a list of fishing-gear items you'd like your grandson to have by the time you go fishing together.

A quality retirement can take five or more years to "transition into," depending on your dreams. Buying a yacht and sailing around the world obviously takes a lot longer than five years to figure out and fund, especially if you're planning to purchase the yacht and learn how to sail. "Read the two hundred books on the Great Books list" is a retirement goal that may take less planning effort, but if you want to own leather-bound editions of those books and have them in place at the outset of your reading campaign, you may need five years.

DREAM ACTIVITY OR EXPERIENCE	STRATEGY OR PLAN FOR IMPLEMENTING THIS DREAM
1. _____	_____ _____ _____ _____ _____
2. _____	_____ _____ _____ _____ _____
3. _____	_____ _____ _____ _____ _____
4. _____	_____ _____ _____ _____ _____
5. _____	_____ _____ _____ _____ _____

6. _____   _____
                      _____
                      _____
                      _____
                      _____

7. _____   _____
                      _____
                      _____
                      _____
                      _____

8. _____   _____
                      _____
                      _____
                      _____
                      _____

9. _____   _____
                      _____
                      _____
                      _____
                      _____

10. _____   _____
                      _____
                      _____
                      _____
                      _____

The point of this exercise is not to completely outline your retirement years but to point out to you that retirement takes PLANNING. Dreams require funding for their implementation. A quality retirement life doesn't just happen. It requires some effort and forethought NOW.

Exercise #58

Retirement Savvy

How smart are you about retirement?

1. According to a *USA Today* report, _____ percent of Americans do not systematically prepare for retirement age by investing.

   a. 41

   b. 56

   c. 62

   d. 74

2. Consumer Federation of America found that of people making less than $35,000 a year, _____ percent said the best way for them to have $500,000 at retirement age is to win the Lotto.

   a. 10

   b. 20

   c. 30

   d. 40

3. A poll conducted by *Wealth Builder* magazine found that _____ percent of Americans believe their standard of living will go UP at retirement.

   a. 80

   b. 65

   c. 50

   d. 35

4. *USA Today* has reported that out of one hundred people age sixty-five, _____ of them can't write a check for $600 (because they don't have the money in their bank accounts or savings).

   a. twenty-seven
   b. forty-eight
   c. seventy-nine
   d. ninety-seven

5. According to a *USA Today* survey, out of one hundred people age sixty-five, _____ were still working.

   a. thirty-eight
   b. forty-seven
   c. fifty-four
   d. sixty-one

6. A *USA Today* survey has reported that out of one hundred people age sixty-five, _____ were financially secure.

   a. three
   b. seventeen
   c. twenty-three
   d. two

7. In the last eight years, bankruptcies among those sixty-five and older have gone up _____ percent.

   a. 54
   b. 98
   c. 137
   d. 164

Answers:

1. (b.) According to a *USA Today* report, 56 percent of Americans do not systematically prepare for retirement age by investing.

2. (d.) Consumer Federation of America found that of people making less than $35,000 a year, 40 percent said the best way for them to have $500,000 at retirement age is to win the Lotto. (Talk about living in a fantasy world!)

3. (a.) A poll conducted by *Wealth Builder* magazine found that 80 percent of Americans believe their standard of living will go UP at retirement. (They are probably in for a very rude and disillusioning awakening.)

4. (d.) *USA Today* has reported that out of one hundred people age sixty-five, ninety-seven of them can't write a check for $600 (because they don't have the money in their bank accounts or savings). (*Note:* That's only $600, not $6,000 or $60,000.)

5. (c.) According to a *USA Today* survey, out of one hundred people age sixty-five, fifty-four were still working.

6. (a.) A *USA Today* survey has reported that out of one hundred people age sixty-five, three were financially secure.

7. (d.) In the last eight years, bankruptcies among those sixty-five and older have gone up 164 percent. (Yikes!)

What we can conclude from the answers in the exercise above is that people who enter their retirement years in our nation are NOT preparing for retirement, are NOT prepared for retirement, and CAN'T HANDLE the expenses of retirement! These are national statistics. They do not need to be YOUR personal statistics if you take action NOW.

Case Study: Two Friends

I have a friend in his forties who has a bodybuilder's physique. He is lean with well-defined muscle groups, but he is not a wild health nut. He watches what he eats and works out a couple of times a week.

I have another friend in his thirties who diets fanatically, runs every day, lifts weights three times a week, but is still forty pounds overweight. He started a health-and-fitness journey a couple of years ago and is losing weight and getting in shape.

The muscle-man friend tells me that he worked hard years ago to get in shape, but he isn't working nearly as hard today.

The Total Money Makeover works in a similar way. Highly focused intensity and effort are required to get to the wealth steps, but once there, simple maintenance can keep your money muscles maintained. Keep in mind that my muscle-man friend never eats three plates of food at a sitting. He still works out and is aware of health issues, and he hasn't forgotten the basic exercising and nutrition principles that got him in excellent shape in the first place. He simply doesn't have to work as hard now to MAINTAIN his fitness level as my friend who is trying to ACHIEVE a fitness level.

Achieving financial fitness is also more difficult than maintaining financial fitness. The rich really do get richer.

Key Concept #2
Invest 15 Percent of Your Income in Retirement

The next step for you to take in the Total Money Makeover is to invest 15 percent of BEFORE-tax gross income annually toward retirement.

Gazellelike intensity in completing the previous steps of the Total

Money Makeover have brought you to the point where you HAVE money to invest in retirement. How did we come up with the 15 percent figure? The number has been derived from working with tens of thousands of people.

Why not more than 15 percent? Because you still have your house to pay off and perhaps college tuition for your children to pay off.

Why not less? Some people want to invest less to pay for college or to pay off their house more quickly. It's wiser to start investing for retirement as SOON AS POSSIBLE so the money has the maximum time to grow. Your children's college degrees won't feed you at retirement. You need some MONEY in retirement to LIVE in a paid-for house. I've counseled too many seventy-five-year-olds who have a paid-for house and no money. They end up selling the family home, or mortgaging it, to eat. That's a bad plan.

In calculating the amount you put into retirement, do NOT include company matches in your plan. If your company matches some or part of your contribution to a retirement plan, consider that gravy.

As a general rule of thumb, if you cheat down to 12 percent or up to 17 percent, that's not a huge problem, but do understand the dangers of straying far from 15 percent. If you underinvest, you may one day be buying that classic cookbook, 72 *Ways to Prepare Alpo and Love It*. If you overinvest, you will keep your home mortgage too long, which will hold up wealth building.

Simple Q & A

Q: According to Automatic Data Processing, Inc., _____ percent of workers would NOT be able to make a mortgage, utility, or credit-card payment if they missed a paycheck.

A: 20

Do NOT use your potential Social Security benefits in your calculations for retirement. I don't count on an inept government for my dignity at retirement, and you shouldn't either. A recent survey revealed that more people under age thirty believe in flying saucers than believe they will receive a dime from Social Security. I agree—not for political reasons, but because the math of that system doesn't work. It spells doom far more than it spells dignity. Now, if by some miracle Social Security is there for you when you retire, consider that also to be gravy.

What About You?

Are you thinking like a gazelle? Are you intensely focused like a gazelle running from Mr. Cheetah?

Exercise #59

Thinking Retirement

Just to reinforce some of these concepts, let's see if you can complete the four statements below correctly. Circle the word, phrase, or number from the options given.

1. Invest **15 / 25** percent of your **after-tax net / before-tax gross** income in retirement funds.

2. **DO / DO NOT** take into consideration any company matching funds as you calculate your retirement investment.

3. **DO / DO NOT** take into consideration Social Security in anticipating your retirement income.

4. Begin investing in retirement **AS SOON AS POSSIBLE / AT LEAST FIVE YEARS BEFORE RETIREMENT.**

Answers:

1. (15, before-tax gross) Invest *15* percent of your BEFORE-TAX gross income in retirement funds. In other words, if you are making $40,000 a year, invest $6,000 a year in your retirement fund.

2. (DO NOT) DO NOT take into consideration any company matching funds as you calculate your retirement investment.

3. (DO NOT) DO NOT take into consideration Social Security in anticipating your retirement income.

4. (AS SOON AS POSSIBLE) Begin investing in retirement AS SOON AS POSSIBLE. You'll never be sorry down the line!

Key Concept #3

Invest for Retirement in Mutual Funds

The Total Money Makeover preferred "investment vehicle" for retirement is "Growth-Stock Mutual Funds." This type of investment fund is good for the long haul. It isn't what I'd recommend for the short-term.

Why growth-stock mutual funds?

Ibbotson Research has reported that 97 percent of the five-year periods in the stock market's history have made money, and 100 percent of the ten-year periods have made money. Mutual funds are a great way for regular people to participate in a great long-term investment like the stock market, even if they want to lower risk and don't have a lot of money to start.

Here's how I approach the investment of retirement funds:

Matching Advantages

Take advantage of any matching programs available to you. Always start where you have a "match." If your company will give you free money, take it! If your 401k matches the first 3 percent you invest, put your first 3 percent of your 15 percent in that fund.

Tax Advantages

Use any tax advantages available. In other words, fund your Roth IRA. A Roth IRA will allow you to invest $3,000, $4,000, or $5,000 a year, per person, depending on which year you read this book. There are some limitations as to income and situation, but most people can invest in a Roth IRA. The Roth grows TAX-FREE. Let me give you a little example of how valuable this can be:

If you invest $3,000 a year from age thirty-five to age sixty-five, and your mutual Roth IRA funds average 12 percent a year over the long haul of those thirty years, you will have $873,000 TAX-FREE at age sixty-five. Over those thirty years, you will have put in only $90,000 . . . the rest is GROWTH and you pay NO taxes.

In a ROTH IRA, you can choose where you put the money. Here's how I choose the Growth-Stock Mutual Funds for my Roth IRA investment:

- I look for a good track record of winning for more than five years, preferably for more than ten years. (I don't look at one-year or three-year track records . . . rather, I think in terms of five-year and ten-year.)
- I break down my retirement investing evenly across four types of funds:
  1. Growth and Income Funds (these are sometimes called Large Cap or Blue Chip Funds).
  2. Growth Funds (these are sometimes called Mid-Cap or Equity funds; an S&P Index Fund would also qualify).
  3. International Funds (these are sometimes called Foreign or Overseas Funds).

4. Aggressive Growth Funds (sometimes called Small-Cap or Emerging Market Funds).

AND THEN . . . The total you put into your matching-fund company retirement plan (401k) and the money you put into Roth IRA funds need to total 15 percent. You may be funding a Roth IRA and be self-employed, or have an income that allows the 15 percent to be greater than a company match plus IRA. In that case, go back and invest the remaining amount up to 15 percent in a 401k, 403b, 457, or SEP (self-employed plan).

Let me give you a real-time example:

Husband earns:	$27,000 a year
Wife earns:	$20,000 a year
Total income:	$47,000 a year

Investment amount of 15 percent would be $7,050 a year.

The husband's 401k matches the first 3 percent. Three percent of his $27,000 income is $810. That goes into the 401k. The wife doesn't work for a company that matches.

The husband and wife each can have a Roth IRA at $3,000 year, for a total of $6,000.

The 401k and Roth IRA amounts added together = $6,810.

There's still $240 to be invested.

Go back to the 401k. Bump the annual husband's contribution to 4 percent instead of 3 percent. That puts $1,080 of his salary into the 401k.

Now the total of 401k and Roth IRA contributions is $7,080. That's at least 15 percent—just $30 above!

NOTE: On the next page you'll find some valuable information about "Retirement Options." Also, if you want a full discussion of what mutual funds are and why I use this mix, go to our Web site at daveramsey.com and visit MyTMMO.

Retirement Options

The changes under the Economic Growth and Tax Relief Reconciliation Act of 2001 affect some retirement plans. The salary-reduction limits are as follows:

YEAR	401K/403B/SAR-SEP	SIMPLE	457
2001	$10,500	$6,500	$8,500
2002	$11,000	$7,000	$11,000
2003	$12,000	$8,000	$12,000
2004	$13,000	$9,000	$13,000
2005	$14,000	$10,000	$14,000
2006	$15,000	$10,000	$15,000
2007 and Following Fully Phased In	Adjusted for Inflation	Adjusted for Inflation	Adjusted for Inflation

There are also new salary-reduction *catch-up* contributions that can be made for those individuals who reach 50 years of age during the plan year.

YEAR	401K/403B/457/SAR-SEP	SIMPLE IRA
2002	$1,000	$500
2003	$2,000	$1,000
2004	$3,000	$1,500
2005	$4,000	$2,000
2006	$5,000	$2,500
2007 and Following	Adjusted for Inflation	Adjusted for Inflation

Also, the Economic Growth and Tax Relief Reconciliation Act of 2001 provides a new IRA annual contribution and catch-up limit for those 50 years old and older.

YEAR	MAXIMUM IRA CONTRIBUTION	ADDITIONAL CATCH-UP
2002–2004	$3,000	$500
2005–2007	$4,000	$500 ($1,000 in 2006–2007)
2008	$5,000	$1,000
AFTER 2008	ADJUSTED FOR INFLATION IN $500 INCREMENTS	$1,000

What About You?

So, what are YOUR retirement investment figures?

Exercise #60

*Calculating for
Retirement Investing*

What is your annual income (personal or family)?
X .15 (15 percent) = $ _____

Amount to be invested (the 15 percent figure above): $ _____
                                                         INVESTMENT DOLLARS

Do you work for a company that matches 401k contributions? If so, at what rate
and amount? How much in real dollars is that? $ _____

Subtract this amount from the INVESTMENT DOLLARS figure above:
                                                         $ _____
                                                         READY FOR ROTH amount

How much can you put into a Roth IRA (personal or combined with spouse)?
                                                         $ _____

Subtract this amount from the READY FOR ROTH figure above:
                                                         $ _____
                                                         STILL TO INVEST amount

The number above is the amount you need to put into a 401k, 403b, 457, or SEP.

Breaking Down Your Investment:

Total amount you are putting into a ROTH IRA: $ _____

X .25 (25 percent) = $ _____

This is how much of your Roth IRA should be put into each of the four types of Growth-Stock Mutual Funds described above.

$ _____ in Growth and Income (Large-Cap, Blue Chip)

$ _____ in Growth (Mid-Cap, Equity, S&P Index)

$ _____ in International (Foreign, Overseas)

$ _____ in Aggressive-Growth (Small-Cap, Emerging Market)

Your company 401k may not allow you to choose among investment options. If it does, you can do a similar calculation for choosing your Growth-Stock Mutual Funds.

If you have another type of retirement fund (such as a SEP account if you are self-employed), calculate:

Total amount you are putting into your Personal RETIREMENT FUND (such as SEP)

$ _____

X .25 (25 percent) = $ _____

This is how much you should allocate to each of the four types of Growth-Stock Mutual Funds within your personal RETIREMENT FUNDING vehicle:

$ _____ in Growth and Income (Large-Cap, Blue Chip)

$ _____ in Growth (Mid-Cap, Equity, S&P Index)

$ _____ in International (Foreign, Overseas)

$ _____ in Aggressive-Growth (Small-Cap, Emerging Market)

When you finish calculating all these stock and 401k investments, go back and check: Did you invest 15 percent of your BEFORE-TAX gross income?

Key Concept #4

*Calculate What It Will
Take for You to Retire*

You set some dreams at the outset of this chapter—experiences and events you hope are part of your retirement years. In addition, you most likely want to maintain your CURRENT standard of living—the same house and neighborhood, same type of transportation, and so forth. The following calculation sheets will help you determine how much you NEED to retire with dignity and security.

Let's run through some basic math.

Although I indicated that the stock market has an OVERALL track record of earning 12 percent a year, for the purposes of calculating retirement, I recommend a person use the figure of 8 percent. You should aim at living off 8 percent. (Actually, this 8 percent is based on your funds earning 12 percent a year and inflation stealing about 4 percent a year. If the rate of inflation turns out to be less, you're better off. If your funds earn more, you're better off. If inflation is higher and your funds earn less, you may need to scramble a little as you near retirement . . . but if you are following the Total Money Makeover fully, you'll be able to do that.)

What About You?

Let's get into real-time planning here . . .

Exercise #61

*How Much in the
Retirement Kitty?*

What income would you like to have each year as your basic "retirement" income? This probably is the annual income you have today: $ _____ A YEAR

To have enough for this amount, you will need a nest egg. Divide the number above by .08 =

$ _____ NEST EGG NEEDED

Now, this nest egg is based on your savings growing at a rate of 12 percent and inflation stealing 4 percent, for a net of 8 percent after inflation. The target nest egg is calculated, therefore, at 8 percent. To get the amount needed, you also need to factor in the number of years you have left to save that amount. A chart labeled "8-Percent FACTOR" follows.

NEST EGG NEEDED $ _____
X FACTOR $ _____
(from 8-Percent FACTOR chart below) $ _____
MONTHLY SAVINGS NEEDED NOW $ _____

8-Percent FACTOR Chart

Select the one that matches your current age. If you wait five or ten years to start retirement investing, you will need to calculate at the age you plan to start investing. (Compare this to your current age, even if you don't think you'll start investing until later. You may change your mind.) Retirement is assumed at sixty-five years of age.

AGE	YEARS TO SAVE	FACTOR
25	40	.000286
30	35	.000436
35	30	.000671
40	25	.001051
45	20	.001698
50	15	.002890
55	10	.005466
60	5	.013610

Do NOT panic if you see that you should have started saving twenty years ago to meet your goal! Do not panic if you can't start saving 15 percent right now. Later steps in the Total Money Makeover will allow you to accelerate your investing while still having a life.

No, don't panic, but DO be concerned enough to start investing for your retirement NOW.

Is it doable? Dream with me for a minute. Joe and Suzy Average are a twenty-seven-year-old couple who make a combined total of $40,816 a year. That, by the way, is the average household income in America according to the last U.S. Census Bureau figures.

They invest $6,000 a year (15 percent) in a Roth IRA—$500 a month. They live with intensity and no debt—things aren't flush for them, but they make it. They have no matching funds from a company. They invest ONLY in the Roth IRA. They don't retire at age sixty-five, but at age sixty-seven.

At age sixty-seven, Joe and Suzy Average will have $5,882,386 TAX-FREE! That's almost $6 million. If they live off the interest on that money, at 8 percent earnings they'll have $470,591 a year to spend.

That's with having the national average income today and not getting a single raise in the next thirty-three years, which is highly unlikely. That's starting at age twenty-seven and putting only $500 a month into a Roth IRA.

It's doable!

If, however, you aren't twenty-seven and aren't making $40,000 a year, don't be totally dejected. Start where you are. Work the steps of the plan. Get out of debt. Have $10,000 in an emergency fund. Start investing for your retirement. And don't delay!

10

Make Sure the Kids Are Fit Too: COLLEGE FUNDING

Total Money Makeover
Progress Check

At this point:

- You are debt-free except your house;
- you have three to six months of expenses (usually about $10,000 minimum) in an emergency fund; and
- you are investing 15 percent of your before-tax GROSS income in retirement funds.

You are on the path toward building wealth. You have your finances under control. You no doubt have a growing sense of security that you

---

Simple Q & A

Q: According to a Gallup poll, _____ percent of those who file for bankruptcy feel "depressed" after going through a bankruptcy.

A: 75

---

have an emergency fund, are debt-free, and are starting to invest in your own GOLDEN years!

This chapter covers Baby Step Five.

Key Concept #1
Help Your Child Get a College Education

Here's a chapter you may not need. Your children may already be past college. Or you may not have children (and won't have children) to send to college.

If, however, you have children who are younger than college age, or you anticipate the possibility that you MIGHT have children (acquiring them either by giving birth, through a marriage, adoption, or from a family member unable to care for them) . . . you need this chapter!

I don't know of any GOOD parent who doesn't want as much or more for their children than what they themselves enjoy in life. In our culture, college is important. I consider it so important that I explained to my children that if they didn't go to college, my wife and I would hire people to do mean things to them until they went. A solid education helps a young person begin his or her adult life and career with much more confidence and quality.

You do need to understand, however, the PURPOSE of a college education before you fund it. There are a number of myths about a college education that you need to confront.

COLLEGE MYTHS include:

- A college degree ensures a job. NO, it doesn't.

- A college degree ensures wealth. NO, it doesn't.

- A college degree proves someone has successfully passed a series of tests. NOT NECESSARILY.

- We all know college-educated people who are broke,
  unemployed, and somehow got a degree without really doing the
  work WE think they should have done to earn the degree.
  College is what a young person makes of it.

College can teach only knowledge—not wisdom. It also doesn't teach attitude, character, perseverance, vision, diligence, or good work habits. Your child has to get those on his own.

I have a college degree. I've been a millionaire starting with nothing TWO times (before I was forty). I attribute 15 percent of that success to a college education, 0 percent to a college DEGREE, and 85 percent to attitude, perseverance, diligence, and vision.

College does offer a young person a unique opportunity for friendships, which can result in networking later. It can provide a knowledge base. It can give your child the "calling card" degree to get him into an interview for a job . . . but it is not the answer to all your child's problems or challenges. It is a luxury in life—not a necessity.

Given all that, I do have some FINANCIAL advice for you once you've decided to fund your child's college education.

Here are Dave's Rules for College:

1. *Research the cost of attending various types of schools.* Find out what your alma mater costs today. Find out what the big state school in your area costs. Find out what smaller state schools cost. Find out what private, smaller schools cost. Compare the costs.

In some areas of study, and in a very few careers, WHERE you attend college matters a great deal. The religious affiliation and the spiritual life at the college may matter to you. But when it comes to academic knowledge, many colleges offer basically the same courses at vastly different prices. "Pedigree" from a name-brand college means less and less in our work culture today. If you're going to go into debt to send your child to a school that will require you to borrow $75,000 extra cash, compared to paying cash for a degree from a much less expensive school, ask yourself why.

Look for some of the differences in costs:

- *Tuition.* This cost is greatly underwritten at state schools.
- *Living and eating off-campus.* The student who lives and eats off-campus pays an AVERAGE of $5,000 more per year. Cafeteria food may not be the greatest, and dorm life may not be all that appealing, but it can save $20,000 over a four-year degree program.

2. *Pay cash.* If you have the cash or a scholarship to cover the expenses—no matter how expensive the school of your choice—by all means, go to the number one school of your choice.

3. *Avoid student loans.* They may seem smart when you are sitting in the financial-aid office, but they stick around for what seems like FOR-EVER. *USA Today* reported in 1992 that 42 percent of students took out loans. Just eight years later, in 2000, 64 percent of students took out loans. Loans are the norm these days—but then, so is being broke. I don't recommend either.

4. *Consider all your options.* Work is good for college students. They tend to value their classroom experience more and party less. You may have relatives near the campus who would like to rent out a room and provide an evening meal for your child. You may want to opt for two years at a community college for general education and then transfer to a bigger or more prestigious school for major courses.

What About You?

Are you ready to send your child to college?

Exercise #62

Gearing Up for College

This is a very short exercise to underscore just one point: According to both *Money* magazine and a CBS MarketWatch report:

1. _____ percent of parents have not saved a dime toward a college education for their children.

    a. 10
    b. 17
    c. 28
    d. 39

2. _____ percent of parents have saved less than $1,000 toward a college education for their children.

    a. 2
    b. 4
    c. 8
    d. 12

3. _____ percent of parents have saved $1,000 to $10,000 toward a college education for their children.

    a. 8
    b. 17
    c. 25
    d. 31

Answers:

1. (d.) Thirty-nine percent of parents have not saved a dime toward a college education for their children.

2. (b.) Four percent of parents have saved less than $1,000 toward a college education for their children.

3. (c.) Twenty-five percent of parents have saved between $1,000 and $10,000 toward a college education for their children.

These figures reported by *Money* magazine an CBS Market Watch indicate that 68 percent of parents with children have saved nothing or next to nothing (even $10,000 is not a lot when dealing with college costs)!

The amount YOU have saved for YOUR child's
college expenses: $ _____

Please note that it is VERY important that you NOT think of your emergency fund as a college fund. If you don't have an emergency fund, you'll think of college as an emergency, but it isn't. If you save for college but don't have an emergency fund, you will raid the college fund to keep the house out of foreclosure when you get laid off. If you save for college while making payments on everything under the sun, well . . . you won't have any money to save for college!

Build a strong foundation for your finances and THEN save for a college fund.

Key Concept #2
Get Smart About ESAs and 529s

College tuition goes up faster than regular inflation. Inflation of goods and services averages about 4 percent a year. Tuition inflation averages about 7 percent. (Baby Life insurance programs average less than 2 percent return a year, savings bonds average about 5 percent, and regular savings accounts and money-market funds can average about 3 percent.)

Some states and colleges offer prepaid college tuition. If tuition goes up 7 percent a year, and you prepay it, you basically make 7 percent on your money and break even. That's not too bad. But if your money is in a decent growth-stock mutual fund averaging 12 percent when invested long-term . . . you haven't been as smart with a prepaid plan as you may have thought. Also consider the possibility that you might move, and the "state" fund you prepaid may not apply to out-of-state tuition.

Here's my recommendation:

The ESA. Fund college, or at least the first step of a college fund, with an Educational Savings Account (ESA) invested in growth-stock mutual funds. The ESA, nicknamed the Education IRA, grows tax-free when it is used for higher education.

The ESA allows you to invest $2,000 a year, per child, if your income is under $200,000 a year. That $2,000 amounts to $166.67 a month. Trust me, if your child is young and you do this right, you'll have college under control; if you wait, $166.67 a month isn't going to be a drop in the bucket. If your income level allows you to do an ESA, do it.

You can invest ESA funds in any mix of funds and change the mix at will. It is a very flexible plan and you have the most control.

If you invest $2,000 a year from birth to age eighteen in prepaid tuition, that would purchase about $72,000 in tuition. In an ESA in mutual funds averaging 12 percent, you would have $126,000 TAX-FREE.

If your child is over age eight when you start an ESA, or you aspire to send your child to a more expensive school or anticipate your gifted child may go on to graduate school . . . the ESA is just a beginning.

The 529. If you need to set aside more than the ESA allows, or your income is more than $200,000 a year, you'll want to look at a 529 plan. These are state plans, but most allow you to use the money at any institution of higher learning (which means you can save in New Hampshire but go to college in Kansas). There are several types of 529 plans—make sure you get the right kind!

One type is called the "life phase" plan, which allows the plan administrator to control the money and move it to more conservative investments as the child ages. These tend to perform poorly (at about 8 percent) because they are very conservative.

Another type is the "fixed portfolio" plan, which sets a fixed percentage of your investment in a group of mutual funds and locks you into that fund until you need the money. You can't move the money, which means if you get into some bad funds, you're stuck with them.

"Flexible plans" allow you to move investments around periodically with a certain "family of funds," a fancy name for a brand of mutual funds. Choose from virtually any mutual fund in the American Funds Group, Vanguard, or Fidelity. This is the only type of 529 I recommend!

What About You?

Is all that clear? Let's see . . .

Exercise #63

College Fund Quiz

Check your understanding of college investment funds:

1. If my child is under eight and I make less than $200,000 a year, the best place for me to start an investment for college is
   a. 529 plan
   b. 401 plan
   c. ESA
   d. IRA
   e. IRS

2. If my child is over age eight, or I make less than $200,000 a year, the best place for me to invest for college is:

    a. 529 Plan

    b. 401 Plan

    c. ESA

    d. IRA

    e. IRS

3. If I anticipate sending my child to an expensive school, and the amount saved under an ESA is not enough, I need to invest in:

    a. 529 Plan

    b. 401 Plan

    c. ESA

    d. IRA

    e. IRS

4. ESA funds should be invested in:

    a. Savings Bonds

    b. Money-Market Funds

    c. Growth-Stock Mutual Funds

    d. Whole-Life Funds for babies, such as the Gerber Fund

    e. Passbook savings account

5. The best type of 529 Plan is:

    a. a "Life Phase" plan

    b. a "Fixed Portfolio" plan

    c. a "Flexible" plan

    d. a plan that requires a child to attend college in the state that provides the fund

Answers:

1. (c.) The ESA is the best place to start investing for college if your child is under age eight and you make less than $200,000 a year.

2. (a.) The 529 plan is where you need to invest if your child is over age eight or you make more than $200,000 a year.

3. (a.) The place to invest if you will need MORE money than the ESA will provide is a 529 plan.

4. (c.) A Growth-Stock Mutual Fund is the best place to invest ESA funds.

5. (c.) A "Flexible" plan allows you to invest in mutual funds of your choice, periodically altering your choice if you find you have your money in a fund that isn't performing very well.

Key Concept #3

Get Creative If You're Running Out of Time!

If you have only a couple of years left before your child starts college, get creative! Consider these options:

- The child could attend a cheaper college.

- The child could live on campus and eat cafeteria food.

- The child could work for a company that will help pay his or her way through college. (Many companies pay tuition for their "adult" employees . . . Ask them to pay in advance and require your child to work for the company for a year or two full-time after graduation. Not all companies will say yes to this plan, but it only takes one that will!)

- Look into companies that have work-study programs that pay a child's tuition in exchange for the child working at night or part-time during the day.

- Check out what the military has to offer. The military isn't for everyone, but some young people get four years of free college education for serving four years in the military.

- Check out the National Guard. It pays a person to go to boot camp one summer between high school and college and then pays for enough tuition and books to get a child through the rest of the time. Of course, the child will serve his or her nation in the National Guard in return.

- Take a high-rejection, high-paying summer sales job. If a young person works really hard in a sales job, he can make great money. I know one young man who made $40,000 selling books in one summer!

- Check into "underserved areas" programs. In these programs, the government will pay for school or pay off student loans, if a student or graduate will agree to work in an "underserved area," typically a rural or inner-city area. Most of these programs are for law and medicine. The programs also apply to nursing and some education degrees.

- Check into unclaimed scholarships. There's more than $4 BILLION a year in unclaimed scholarships. Some of these are smaller scholarships from community clubs. Some are based on race, sex, or religion. Some are for highly specialized "traits" in a student. I know one young woman who applied for a thousand of these scholarships. She was turned down for 970 of them, but she got thirty of them totaling $38,000! Software programs are available that cover more than three hundred thousand of these scholarships. Think of searching out these scholarships as a part-time job, or a summer job between the child's junior and senior years of high school.

What About You?

How creative are you? How motivated are you to pay for college in CASH rather than take out student loans?

Exercise #64

Paying for College

List three things you—or your high school student—can look into TODAY for funding college, beyond an ESA or 529 plan:

1. _____

2. _____

3. _____

11

Be Ultrafit:
PAY OFF THE HOME MORTGAGE

Total Money Makeover
Progress Check

At this point:

- You are debt-free except your house;
- you have three to six months of expenses (usually about $10,000 minimum) in an emergency fund;
- you are putting 15 percent of your before-tax gross income into retirement savings each year; and
- you are investing for your child's college education.

If you are doing this, you are among the top 5 to 10 percent of all Americans because you have some wealth, have a plan, and have your finances under control! It's time to press on through!

This chapter covers Baby Step Six.

Key Concept #1

*Start an Accelerated Payment
Plan to Pay Off Your House Loan*

For many people, the largest single "payment" they have every month is a house mortgage (or condominium mortgage). Imagine what it would be like not to have that payment! Imagine what you could begin to do with that money in terms of investing, making contributions, or just plain ol' having fun!

The principle behind this step in the Total Money Makeover is that EVERY dollar you can find in your budget above basic living, retirement investing, and college funding should be put into making extra payments on your home. Again, I challenge you to attack that home mortgage with gazellelike INTENSITY!

There are lots of myths associated with home mortgages. Let's take them on!

What About You?

Do you feel a special excitement about the possibility of owning your own home? Hold on to that excitement. You're RIGHT to be excited about that possibility!

Simple Q & A

Q: According to the Federal Reserve Board, consumers' outstanding debt on credit cards and other revolving loans has grown continuously over the last decade, hitting $ _____ last year.

A: $1.5 TRILLION

Exercise #65

Managing a Home Mortgage Wisely

Check below whether you think each statement below is a MYTH or the TRUTH:

MYTH TRUTH

❑ ❑   1. It is wise to keep my home mortgage to get a tax deduction.

❑ ❑   2. I should borrow the maximum amount I can on my home (refinancing to get cash out) because of the great interest rates right now—and then invest the money at a high rate.

❑ ❑   3. It's smart to take out a thirty-year mortgage and then pay on it as if it's a fifteen-year mortgage.

❑ ❑   4. A fifteen-year mortgage is better than a thirty-year mortgage.

❑ ❑   5. It's better to have a fixed-rate mortgage, even if the rate is higher, than to have an adjustable-rate mortgage (ARM) or balloon mortgage.

❑ ❑   6. I would be smart to take out a home-equity loan as my "emergency fund."

❑ ❑   7. Now is a great time to refinance my home.

Answers:

1. (MYTH) There's nothing wise about keeping a home mortgage just to get a tax deduction. Tax deductions are no bargain!

     Let's do some simple math. If you have a home payment of around $900, and the interest part of that is $830 a month, you have paid around $10,000 that year in interest. That's your "tax deduction." The bank or other lending organization gets your $10,000.

     On the other hand, if you have a debt-free home, that $10,000 is part of your income, and you'll have to pay tax on it. If you are in about the 30-percent bracket, you'll pay about $3,000 on that income. You'll still have $7,000 to spend as you want.

It doesn't make any sense to me to send $10,000 in interest to a bank so you don't have to send $3,000 to the IRS.

2. (MYTH) It is NOT wise to borrow the maximum amount you can borrow on your home (refinancing to get cash out) in hopes of investing that money in something that has a high interest rate. The truth is, you really don't make anything when the smoke clears.

This can be a little complicated, so stay with me. I know you can!

The myth-speakers claim it's smart to borrow money at around 8 percent to invest it in a 12-percent mutual fund.

Let's try that myth on real dollars.

Let's say you borrow $100,000 on your home to invest. If you borrowed the money in the first place at 8 percent, you paid $8,000 on that amount in your mortgage. If you invest the $100,000 at 12 percent, you'll make $12,000. The difference is $4,000 . . . or is it?

If you're in the 30-percent tax bracket, you'll pay $3,600 in taxes at ordinary income rates, or $2,400 if you invest at capital gains rates. You won't net $4,000. More like $400 to $1,600 . . . so far . . . but there's more to consider.

If I, as your next-door neighbor, have $100,000 equity in my home that you don't have because you took it out to "invest," which one of us is more secure? If you get sick, have a car wreck, or are downsized out of a job, you can run into major problems with an extra $100,000 on your mortgage. Debt has caused your RISK to increase. The money you have in your mortgage is not at risk.

If you take into consideration both taxes and risk, you don't REALLY come out ahead.

3. (MYTH) The idea behind taking out a thirty-year mortgage and promising to pay yourself as if it's a fifteen-year mortgage is that you will have some wiggle room IF something goes wrong. In all likelihood, something WILL go wrong.

The truth is, very few people have the discipline to pay on a thirty-year mortgage as if it's a fifteen-year mortgage. The FDIC reports that 97.3 percent of people do NOT systematically pay EXTRA on their mortgage. Never take more than a fifteen-year mortgage. One thing I've noticed through the years is that fifteen-year mortgages tend to get paid in fifteen years. Thirty-year mortgages tend to get paid in thirty years.

4. (TRUE) A fifteen-year mortgage will save you considerable dollars over a thirty-year mortgage every time. The shorter the term of a loan, the less interest paid! Let me give you an example.

Let's assume that Bob and Ann buy a $130,000 house. They make a down payment of $20,000, which leaves them a $110,000 mortgage.

If a mortgage loan is at 7 percent, at the end of thirty years, they will have paid a total of $263,520 for their $130,000 house.

At the same interest rate, but at the end of fifteen years, they will have paid $177,840 for their $130,000 house.

That's a difference of $85,680! That money invested for the extra fifteen years (the difference in years between the fifteen-year mortgage and the thirty-year mortgage) can be TREMENDOUS!

"But," you say, "there's a big difference in monthly payments."

Bob and Ann would pay $732 a month in a thirty-year loan.

They would pay $988 a month in a fifteen-year loan. That's $256 a month—which isn't a lot for most people if they are DEBT-FREE.

Plus, these figures are calculated at the same 7-percent interest rate for both loans. Fifteen-year loans are often at a lower interest rate than thirty-year loans, which would make the difference each month less than $256.

With interest rates low, it may be a great time to refinance your home at a fifteen-year rate if you have more than fifteen years to pay on your existing mortgage.

If you have a VERY low interest rate (lower than the going rate), or you have less than fifteen years to pay on a mortgage, you may pay off your mortgage at significant savings by paying off your mortgage faster.

I have a mortgage payoff calculator chart on my Web site, daveramsey.com, where you can calculate different payments or even run an amortization schedule.

5. (TRUE) It is better to have a fixed rate mortgage, even if the rate is higher, than to have an adjustable-rate mortgage (ARM) or balloon mortgage. The main argument used to try to get you to buy an ARM or balloon mortgage is probably this: "If you'll be moving in a few years anyway, this is the better deal." The truth is that you will be moving—when they foreclose!

Adjustable Rate Mortgages (ARMs) were invented in the early 1980s. Prior to that, all of us in the real estate business were selling fixed-rate mortgages at 7 and 8 percent. The economy went south, and mortgages suddenly skyrocketed to 17 percent. The real estate world froze. Lenders were paying out 12 percent on certificates of deposit, but had money loaned out at 7 percent on mortgages—multiply that fact by millions of dollars in mortgages and CDs, and you see the problem! The ARM was born so interest rates would go up as the prevailing market interest rates rose. The risk was transferred from the lending organizations (banks and such) to YOU, the consumer.

It is never wise to get something that adjusts when you are at the bottom of rates . . . and that's where we are in 2003. The ARM will go UP as interest rates go up.

Balloon mortgages are worse. People who think they are going to move BEFORE the balloon mortgage kicks in are often very surprised at how fast that five-year balloon note comes due! Balloons tend to pop.

6. (MYTH) A home-equity loan becomes a DEBT. The very time you DON'T need more debt is when you have an emergency!

The home-equity loan is one of the most aggressively marketed loans today. It plays into our I-want-it-now mind-set as a culture. By the way, the banking industry calls these loans HELs for short . . . I think they just left off an *L*.

Most HELs are renewable annually, meaning that you must requalify for this loan once a year. If you have a major emergency during that time, you may very well lose your house if you have borrowed a significant amount against it and then lose your job or have a serious car wreck that not only demolishes your car but lands you in the hospital. Most of the time, the very emergency that causes you to use the home-equity loan is the one that will cause you NOT to be able to qualify for the annual renewal. "Step up on this rug so we can pull it out from under you."

7. (Maybe MYTH, Maybe TRUE) I don't know when "NOW" is—as in, I don't know when you are reading this or making this argument. I can tell you this about refinancing . . .

The best time to refinance is when you can save on interest. The charts on the following pages can help you decide if now is the time.

Should I Refinance?
How to Figure the Change in Your ARM

When refinancing, paying points or origination fees is NOT in your best interest. Points or origination fees are prepaid interest. When you pay points, you get a lower Annual Percentage Rate (APR) because you've already paid some of the interest up front. When I have calculated the money that points save, and used that to pay me back for the points, it averages about ten years to get my money back. The Mortgage Bankers Association says the average life of a mortgage is only about 5.6 years, so on average you don't save enough to get your money back before you pay off the loan by moving or refinancing. When refinancing, ask for a "par" quote, which means zero points and a zero origination fee. The mortgage broker can make a profit by selling the loan. They don't need the origination fee to be profitable.

Case Study: Marathon Man!

I have a good friend who runs marathons. I listen in awe to his stories of the marathons he has run. To a guy who sees 2.6 miles as a real daily accomplishment, the very idea of running 26.2 miles is nearly

How to Figure Your New Payment

Monthly Payment per $1,000 in Loan Amount

Rate	15-Year	30-Year
4.5%	7.65	5.07
5.0%	7.91	5.37
5.5%	8.17	5.68
6.0%	8.44	6.00
6.5%	8.71	6.32
7.0%	8.99	6.66
7.5%	9.28	7.00
8.0%	9.56	7.34
8.5%	9.85	7.69
9.0%	10.15	8.05
9.5%	10.44	8.41
10.0%	10.75	8.78
10.5%	11.05	9.15
11.0%	11.37	9.52
11.5%	11.68	9.90
12.0%	12.00	10.29

_____ \ 1,000 = _____ X _____ = _____

Sales Price \ 1,000 = #1,000's X Rate = Monthly Pymt

Example: Sales Price - $90,000, 15 years at 8%

$90,000 \ 1,000 = 90 X 9.56 (look at rate and # of years financed) =

$860.40 Monthly Payment

Should I Refinance?

Current Principal and Interest Payment _____
(without taxes & insurance)

New Principal and Interest Payment (minus) _____

Equals Monthly Savings _____

_____ / _____ = _____

Total Closing Costs Divided by Savings = Number of Months to Break Even.

Example: Refinance on a $90,000 mortgage

$1,100 current payment - $950 new payment = $150 savings
$1,950 closing costs divided by $150 savings = 13 months

Will you stay in your home longer than the number of months to break even? If so, you are a candidate for a refinance.

ESTIMATED CLOSING COSTS TABLE

Loan Amount	Closing Costs	Loan Amount	Closing Costs
30,000	1,500	35,000	1,550
40,000	1,600	45,000	1,650
50,000	1,700	55,000	1,725
60,000	1,775	65,000	1,800
70,000	1,825	75,000	1,850
80,000	1,900	85,000	1,925
90,000	1,950	95,000	1,975
100,000	2,000	150,000	2,300
200,000	2,600	250,000	2,900

How to Figure
the Change in Your ARM

Your Adjustable Rate Mortgage adjusts based on the movement of an index. You can find your index in your original note or mortgage. The most commonly used index is the Treasury Bill. The one-year ARM uses the one-year T-Bill, and the three-year ARM uses the three-year T-Bill, and so on. Other commonly used indexes are the LIBOR and THE 11TH DISTRICT COST OF FUNDS.

First, find out what index you use and when it is adjusted.

Next, find out (also from your paperwork) what "margin" was assigned to your loan (usually 2.59).

Basically your ARM moves as the index moves.

The index is usually published daily in the *Wall Street Journal.*

So if you have a one-year ARM that adjusts with the one-year T-Bill and a margin of 2.59 (which is typical), then at the one-year anniversary of your closing you would look up the one-year T-Bill in the *Wall Street Journal.* Add the T-Bill to your margin, and you have your new rate (if it is not capped).

Example: T-Bill 4.41 plus margin 2.59 = 7% new interest rate.

Warning: Almost all ARMs start below margin the first year, guaranteeing a payment increase at anniversary unless rates DROP.

overwhelming. Marathoners are among the most physically fit people on the planet.

In the realm of finances, those who own their homes are like experienced marathon runners!

My marathon-running friend tells me that marathoners often hit a "wall" at about the eighteen-mile mark. Nasty things begin to happen to their muscles and mind. My friend said, "You begin to think things like, *Eighteen miles is pretty good. Few people can accomplish that.* If you aren't careful, the 'good enough' thinking becomes the enemy of finishing."

That's good wisdom to remember when it comes to paying off your house.

Key Concept #2
If at All Possible, Pay Cash for Your House

I've actually had people tell me they didn't know it was POSSIBLE to pay cash for a house. Trust me, it is!

Now, let me quickly tell you that I am not opposed to a person's having a home mortgage. It is the only kind of debt I don't yell about, in part because a house is generally an investment that increases in value rather than decreases, in part because a house generally gives a person a feeling of security and well-being, and in part because houses are expenses, and it's very rare that a person can pay cash for a house at the outset.

What I DO tell people is that they should never take more than a fifteen-year, fixed-rate loan, and that their payment should never be more than 25 percent of their take-home pay.

As for me personally, I don't borrow money . . . ever. My wife, Sharon, and I have what we call "The 100-Percent-Down Plan." We pay cash.

In my experience, I've found that families who stay gazellelike intense on paying off a mortgage achieve that goal in about seven years from the date they begin a Total Money Makeover.

That isn't what RICH people do. It's what ordinary couples do. One couple told me they had an annual $70,000 income. When they started their Total Money Makeover, they had $20,000 in student loans, $10,000 in car loans, $3,000 in credit-card debt, and a $85,000 mortgage—a grand total of $118,000 in debt. But in SIX YEARS, they had paid off every cent!

Simple Q & A

Q: *The Consumer Reports Money Book* says the typical household has $ _____ in debt.

A: $38,000

I've seen it done thousands of times by ordinary people with an extraordinary desire. They are people who are willing to live now like nobody else lives . . . so they can live later like nobody else!

What About You?

Are you willing to live like nobody else now . . . so later you can live like nobody else?

Case Study: Luke

I had a caller named Luke one day. He started his plan at twenty-three years old, making $50,000 a year. He married a young woman making $30,000 a year. He and his bride lived in a small apartment over a rich lady's garage—they paid only $250 a month for the apartment. They chose to live on next to nothing, did virtually nothing that cost money, and they SAVED. They saved with gazellelike intensity! They were able to save $50,000 each year for three years, and they paid CASH for a $150,000 home. They closed on the home on Luke's wife's twenty-sixth birthday.

Luke's family and friends thought he should be committed—they made fun of his cars, his lifestyle, and his dream. They DIDN'T make fun of Luke when he paid cash for such a beautiful home.

You may not make as much money as Luke and his bride. It may take you five years of sacrifice . . . or seven . . . to pay cash for a home. On the other hand, you may not need a $150,000 house as a starter home. Ask any eighty-year-old if five years of sacrifice is worth the satisfaction of knowing you have changed your financial destiny for the rest of your life, and I doubt if you'll hear a "no" answer.

Exercise #66

Paying Off the House

Take a look at your monthly budget. Assuming by now that you have no debt to pay in your monthly budget, you have an emergency fund in place, you have already allocated 15 percent to retirement, and you are funding or have already funded a college fund for your children, how much money can you set aside every month to pay against the PRINCIPAL of your mortgage?

$ _____ a month that can be paid against the principal on the home mortgage

Take a look at your mortgage statement. What do you still owe on your home in PRINCIPAL?

$ _____ principal still outstanding.

Divide what you still owe in principal by the amount you can set aside each month to pay on the principal. How many months away are you from payment-free HOME OWNERSHIP?

_____ months of paying until the home is FULLY YOURS!

12

Arnold Schwarzedollar, Mr. Universe of Money: BUILD WEALTH LIKE CRAZY

Total Money Makeover
Progress Check

At this point:

- You are completely debt-free;
- you have three to six months of expenses (usually about $10,000 minimum) in an emergency fund;
- you are putting 15 percent of your before-tax gross income into retirement savings each year;
- you are investing in or have fully funded your child's college education; and
- you have a fully paid-for house.

You are not Mastered by a Card . . . you have not Discovered bondage . . . American Excess has left your life . . . you have no student loans . . . you have no house payment and no car payment. You are FREE! You live on a monthly written plan, and your retirement destiny is looking considerably better than living on Alpo and Social Insecurity. You are on the brink of WEALTH.

This is Baby Step Seven.

Key Concept #1

Taking on the Responsibility
of Being a Wealthy Person

I realize it's fairly late in the game to be asking, but what was your purpose in having a Total Money Makeover? Why did you do it? Why all the sacrifice and work? Why go to all this trouble and effort?

For that matter, why does a person want to be healthy? A person may lose weight, build up his cardiovascular system, trade in fat for muscle . . . but why? Just so you can have abs, pecs, and quads? No, a person chooses to become fit because it feels GOOD to be fit, and because being fit gives a person energy, greater quality of life, and more "zest" for having fun, going places, trying new physical activities, and being around other people.

Why does a person want to be debt-free and pursue wealth? It takes a lot less self-control, a lot less sacrifice, and a lot less time, creativity, and effort to live in debt. Wealth doesn't answer all life's questions, make you trouble-free, or give you self-esteem. Wealth is not an escape mechanism. So what is it that you thought would be a good idea?

After years of studying, teaching, and even preaching on this subject across America, I can find only three good uses for money:

1. Money is good for FUN.

2. Money is good to INVEST.

3. Money is good to GIVE.

Anything else you can think of to do with wealth probably doesn't reflect good mental or spiritual health.

What About You?

Why do you aspire to live a debt-free, wealthy life?

Exercise #67

Fun, Fun, Fun

Reflect for a moment on the statement "Money is good for FUN," and then write down your first thoughts in response. Do you truly believe it's okay to have FUN with money? Do you believe it's acceptable to buy something you'd really like to own, even though others might call such a purchase ridiculous?

If your bills are paid . . . you are giving what you feel you should give . . . you are invested for retirement to the degree you want to be invested . . . you have no debt . . . why not have fun?

Here are some ideas to consider:

- A cruise with your family or a family trip to a faraway place with a strange-sounding name
- A new car with all the bells and whistles you've ever dreamed about
- A shopping spree to Paris or New York City
- An ORIGINAL painting or sculpture by your favorite artist
- A large diamond ring
- A boat in the harbor with the name of your choice on its backside

List three things you think it would be FUN to own or do:

1. _____

2. _____

3. _____

The trouble with having FUN with money is that the people who generally believe it's fine to have fun are people who can't afford the fun stuff they want to own or do!

There have been days on my talk show when about 70 percent of the people I assisted were having difficulty deciding what to do about the luxury car they had purchased. The high car payment was keeping them from paying off their other debts. It was keeping them from stashing away money in an emergency fund. I once joked that I perhaps should rename my talk radio show *The Sell the Car Show*. Why is this the case in our nation? Because people think having a new luxury car will give them prestige, and that it will be FUN to own the car of their dreams. They don't realize their dream is actually a scheme—a scheme that keeps them in the bondage of debt to the point that all other goals and dreams pale in the red-hot glare of a MONTHLY PAYMENT for four wheels and a ton of steel.

At times people seem to wander blindly into the snare of a purchase for something they "just had to have." In truth, they didn't need it at all.

Case Study: Michael

I had a call one day from a man named Michael who asked me if he should buy a Harley-Davidson motorcycle. They are fabulous bikes, but they are not for broke people. A nice one costs well over $20,000.

Given my experiences over the years with people who want luxury items they can't truly afford, I jumped to the conclusion at the outset that Michael was twenty-eight years old, making about $48,000 a year with two car payments, two kids, one wife, and no money. I thought he probably was having a little-boy fantasy about having fun, and I was all prepared to tell him to straighten out his thinking and grow up.

For a few minutes I talked about how great Harleys are and how a lot of guys love to have one. Then I asked Michael what he made last year, figuring I'd have him on the ropes. He said, "$650,000."

I gulped, and then, figuring maybe he had come into a special windfall, I asked, "Yeah, but what have you averaged over the last five years." He said, "About $550,000 a year."

"How much do you have in investments?" I asked.

"About $20 million."

I had only four words of advice for him. "Buy the Harley, dude!"

I see absolutely nothing wrong with a man enjoying a fun item he wants to purchase when it is a percentage of his wealth that would equal a Happy Meal for most other people. He has earned his Harley and then some.

Key Concept #2
Continue to Make Wise Investments

You'll probably find that the more you make money, the more you enjoy the process of investing money. Investing will become a little like a game to you. The market fluctuates, but as mature investors, you ride the waves. Surfing is fun for those who know how to do it and enjoy the process—not every wave is a good one, but the overall average on a day is usually a positive experience!

Here are Dave's Basic Rules of Investing:

1. Until you have more than $10 million invested, *keep your investing very simple*. You can clutter your life with a bunch of unnecessary stress if you get involved in extremely complex investments. I use simple mutual funds and debt-free real estate as my investment mix. It's very clean, simple, and has some tax advantages.

2. *Always manage your own money*. You may surround yourself with a team of people who are smarter than you about money, but YOU make the decisions. (You can tell if they are smarter than you if they can explain complex issues in ways you can understand them. In other words, if a financial adviser is

difficult to understand, he isn't smarter than you.) Always keep in mind that God did not give your financial advisers the responsibility for the money you have . . . He gave that responsibility to you. I've seen celebrities and professional athletes lose their entire fortunes because they gave up the responsibility of managing their own money.

3. *Build a team of advisers.* The Bible says, "In the multitude of counselors there is safety" (Prov. 11:14). I believe that! A good estate-planning attorney, a CPA or tax expert, an insurance pro, an investment pro, and a good realtor are a few of the essential team members you should have. I endorse the use of a Financial Planner if that person is a team member and not the entire team, or even the captain of the team. Choose people who have the heart of a teacher, not the heart of either a salesman or an "expert." The "salesman" will always be chasing a commission and thinking short-term. The "expert" can't help but be condescending (which is ironic since he has less money than you do).

What About You?

Who is on your team of financial advisers?

Exercise #68

Who's on Your Team?

Name your financial team of advisers:

Estate-Planning Attorney _____

CPA or Tax Expert _____

Insurance Expert _____

Realtor _____

Financial Planner _____

If you don't have this team in place, give some thought as to whom you'd like to have on this team. Also give some thought as to what point in your overall wealth-building game plan you believe you need to bring that expert on board.

Key Concept #3
Aim for the Pinnacle Point

I grew up in the suburbs in Tennessee, so I was accustomed to riding a bike up and down hills. To a seven-year-old with a one-gear bicycle, a huge hill looked like Mount Everest. I quickly learned the technique of "switch-back." Instead of pedaling straight up, I would painfully bike from side to side, taking a small bite at a time out of a Tennessee mountain. At times the heat seemed ovenlike, the beads of sweat turned into rivers, and I'm sure my face was like a Halloween mask with all the strain and determination I etched into it as I climbed the hill. Push, push, breathe, breathe, pedal, pedal . . . until I finally reached the crest of the hill.

Finally, there I stood at the Pinnacle Point. It was a perfect moment to savor. All the sweat, work, and pain were worth it because ahead was the RIDE DOWN. It was glorious! The wind was in my hair, and my feet were no longer on the pedals but on the handlebars. The *click, click, click* of the baseball cards in the spokes was like the chattering of a thousand crickets. The wind tickled my ears, whispering, "You're the king!" It was a wonderful feeling of accomplishment and pure pleasure!

What's the joy in investing? When you save and invest and finally reach the Pinnacle Point.

What's the Pinnacle Point? The place where you have invested to the point that you can live off 8 percent of your nest egg. (You calculated that number in a previous exercise in the chapter on retirement investing.)

When you can live off 8 percent of your nest egg, your money is making more than you do!

And believe me, the downhill ride is worth the effort!

What About You?

Go back to Chapter 9 and review the information in Exercises #60 and #61. What's YOUR Pinnacle Point?

Exercise #69

Getting to Your Pinnacle Point

Consult the chart below.

- Determine how many years you have to retirement . . . or to the place you'd like to set as your Pinnacle Point.
- Determine how much you have to invest each month to get there.

At your current rate of investing, how long will it be before you reach the Pinnacle Point?

Are you willing to invest more each month? YES / NO

MONTHLY DEBT PAYMENTS ROB YOU OF YOUR RETIREMENT

Years Invested Monthly at 12% Per Year

Monthly Payments	5	10	15	25	40
$100	8,167	23,004	49,958	187,885	1,176,477
$200	16,334	46,008	99,916	375,769	2,352,954
$300	24,500	69,012	149,874	563,654	3,529,431
$400	32,668	92,015	199,832	751,538	4,705,909
$500	40,835	115,019	249,790	939,423	5,882,386
$600	49,002	138,023	299,748	1,127,308	7,058,863
$700	57,168	161,027	349,706	1,315,193	8,235,341
$800	65,336	184,031	399,664	1,503,077	9,411,818
$900	73,503	207,034	449,622	1,690,962	10,588,295
$1,000	81,669	230,039	499,580	1,878,847	11,764,772
$1,200	98,004	276,046	599,496	2,254,616	14,117,727
$1,500	122,504	345,058	749,370	2,818,270	17,647,159
$2,000	163,339	460,077	999,160	3,757,693	23,529,545

Exercise #70

Wealth Quiz

See how many of the following statements you can complete without consulting the Word Pool.

1. When your money makes more than you do, you are officially _____.

2. Build a "wealth team" of _____, but don't give them the responsibility over your funds.

3. Wealth is not an _____ (two words). It is a

   _____ .

4. _____ manage your own money.

5. Choose people for your financial team who are smarter than you but who can explain complex issues in ways you can _____ .

6. Always ask if the person giving you advice will _____ personally from the advice.

7. When you can comfortably live on your investment income, you are

   _____ _____ (two words).

8. You have reached the Pinnacle Point when you can live off _____ percent of your nest egg.

9. Remember, "In the _____ of counselors there is safety" (Prov. 11:14).

10. Build your way to the Pinnacle Point with investments that are simple, clean, and that have _____ (two words).

Word Pool

escape mechanism • wealthy • multitude • understand • advisers
financially secure • 8 • responsibility • profit • always • tax advantages

Answers:

1. wealthy
2. advisers
3. escape mechanism; responsibility
4. always
5. understand

6. profit
7. financially secure
8. 8
9. multitude
10. tax advantages

Go back and read each of these statements aloud with the blanks filled in correctly.

Key Concept #4

Giving Is the Biggest Reward

Without a doubt, I find that the best part of having money is giving it away. It is the MOST fun I have with money.

Luxuries are fun, but after a while, gourmet dining gets old, even luxury cars have troubles, vacations can be exhausting, and golf scores never get so good that they cease to become frustrating.

Investing is fun, but after a while, it becomes a little routine and no longer sets off bells and whistles in your soul.

Giving is fun that doesn't quit.

I have met literally thousands of millionaires in my life, and the ones who are mentally, emotionally, and spiritually healthy all share one thing in common—a love of GIVING.

Only the strong can help the weak, and that is true for money, too. A toddler isn't allowed to carry a newborn—only adults with muscular strength should carry babies and children. The same is true in the material realm. Those who are strong financially are the ones called upon to help those who are weak, injured, or incapable of caring for themselves.

What About You?

Does the idea of giving to help others excite you? If your answer is "No," then maybe you just haven't given enough to unleash that flow of excitement lying dormant within you!

Simple Q & A

Q: According to Christian Financial Concepts, in 1929 only 2 percent of homes in America had a mortgage against them. In 1962, only _____ percent did NOT have a mortgage against them.

A: 2

Exercise #71

Who Gets Your Giving?

List below three organizations or causes you would like to help substantially with finances:

1. _____

2. _____

3. _____

List below three individuals you would like to help with monetary gifts so they might get over a particular hurdle in their life:

1. _____

2. _____

3. _____

Isn't it FUN to think about helping these individuals, organizations, or causes?

Exercise #72

Giving Quiz

Here's a little quiz about some matters related to giving. See how well you do before you consult the Word Pool.

1. Money gives power to good _____ .
2. "No one would have remembered the good Samaritan if he hadn't had
    _____ " (Margaret Thatcher).
3. Givers often report having more fun than those who _____ their gifts.
4. Only the _____ can help the weak.
5. Nothing robs a person's sense of freedom quite like _____ .

Word Pool

money • strong • intentions • greed • receive

Answers:

1. (intentions) Money gives power to good INTENTIONS.
2. (money) Margaret Thatcher once said, "No one would have remembered the good Samaritan if he hadn't had MONEY."

3. (receive) Givers often report having more fun than those who RECEIVE their gifts. Surveys have shown that the old proverb is true: It IS more blessed to give than to receive.

4. (strong) Only the STRONG can help the weak.

5. (greed) Nothing robs a person's sense of freedom quite like GREED. Trust me on this. I've met a lot of greedy people, and every one of them was MISERABLE. Every one of them felt shackled by their intense inner desire to acquire more and more and more.

Key Concept #5

Strike a Balance Among Having Fun, Investing, and Giving

When you reach the Pinnacle Point in your wealth building, strike a balance among the three uses for money: FUN, INVESTING, and GIVING. Do some of each.

Simple Q & A

Q: *USA Today* has reported that Citibank, the largest issuer of Visa cards, will spend $100 million this year just on marketing their credit cards to _____ .

A: high school and college students

Someone who never has fun with money misses the point.

Someone who never invests money will never have MORE with which to have fun or MORE to give.

Someone who never gives will have no real, lasting joy or a sense of fulfillment and purpose from their money.

If you are married, make sure you and your spouse strike an agreement about how you will handle your wealth. My wife, Sharon, is a natural saver, so she always moves toward INVESTING. I'm a natural spender, so I make sure we have FUN. We both enjoy GIVING.

Push the pedals one more round. Switchback if you have to. Keep moving upward, no matter the sweat. I promise you, the top of the hill has a fabulous view, and the ride down is glorious.

What About You?

Are you committed to reaching the Pinnacle Point? Are you excited about the thrill of the ride down the hill and all that you'll be able to do with your wealth?

Exercise #73

Talk It Over

This exercise requires you to have a conversation with your spouse. Discuss the balance YOU want to have in your lives regarding your money as you build wealth. How do each of you feel about

- Money being used for FUN?
- Money being INVESTED?
- Money being GIVEN AWAY?

---- 13 ----

Live Like No One Else:
REACH THE PINNACLE POINT

Total Money Makeover
Progress Check

If you are like most people I encounter in the day-to-day routine of my life, you began this Total Money Makeover workbook a little skeptical and yet hopeful. You probably felt financially flabby and out of shape—overweight with debt and without any "muscle" of savings or investments.

If you have worked all the steps . . . you are no longer in that sad shape.

At this point:

- You are debt-free;

- you have three to six months of expenses (usually about $10,000 minimum) in an emergency fund;

- you are putting 15 percent of your before-tax gross income into retirement savings each year;

- you are investing or have funded your child's college education;

- you own your home; and

- you are building wealth and are on your way to reaching the Pinnacle Point, where you can live off 8 percent of your investments.

If you follow this system, it *will* work. It's a "proven plan"—proven not just by me but by tens of thousands of people who have worked the plan and continue to work it. It is a plan that will work so well, you are going to become wealthy over the next twenty to forty years if you follow this plan.

There's a danger in that, and it's what I want to address in this final chapter.

Key Concept #1
Don't Fall Victim to "Affluenza"

Author Randy Alcorn says in *The Treasure Principle* that "Affluenza" is an ailment that strikes those who begin to seek happiness, solace, and fulfillment in their consumption of STUFF. They begin to place so much priority on their money that they are "ruled" by its management. They become just as much ruled by "stuff"—including an investments portfolio—as a person who is debt-ridden. As Antoine Rivaroli has said, "There are men who gain from their wealth only the fear of losing it."

You may have assumed somewhere along the line in doing the exercises in this workbook that I believe wealth and "stuff" to be the answer to happiness, emotional well-being, and spiritual maturity. If that is your conclusion, you are wrong. I know that isn't the case. To the contrary, I see a real spiritual danger in having great wealth. The danger is old-fashioned materialism.

Materialism is the concept at the heart of the bumper sticker that proclaims, "He who dies with the most toys wins." I like the new bumper sticker that says, "He who dies with the most toys is still dead." Stuff is wonderful. I hope you get some good stuff in your life to enjoy and give away. But I strongly encourage you: Don't let the pursuit of wealth become your god.

My wife, Sharon, and I are concerned that our wealth be a blessing and not a curse to our children. We are tough on our kids regarding work, saving, giving, and spending. We expect a lot from them and have since they were very young. I'm proud of the character of our children. They aren't perfect, but they are doing well. The same is true for us as their parents. True character regarding money is knowing that wealth is not the answer to life's questions. Wealth bears great responsibility.

What About You?

What character issues do you associate with wealth?

Exercise #74

Lasting Character

What character qualities do you believe to be important; stated another way, what character qualities do you want to develop in your life and never lose? Write out those character qualities here:

_____	_____
_____	_____
_____	_____
_____	_____
_____	_____
_____	_____

What do you believe to be the character qualities you would NEVER exchange for wealth?

Discuss these traits with your spouse and other members of your family.

Name several things you and your spouse believe you can and must do to instill these character traits in your children:

_____

_____

_____

_____

Key Concept #2

Realize Wealth Will Make You More of What You Are

A paradox of wealth is that it makes you more of what you are. Let that soak in for a moment. If you are a jerk and you become wealthy, you will become king of the jerks. If you are generous and you become wealthy, you will be most generous! If you are kind, your wealth will allow you to express kindness in immeasurable ways. If you feel guilty, wealth ensures you will feel exceedingly guilty for the rest of your life.

If you are greedy, wealth will make you a misery to everybody around you.

As a Christian, I am amazed at how many people think money is the root of all evil. That isn't what the New Testament teaches. It teaches that the LOVE of money, not money itself, is the root of all evil. (If you question me on this, go read 1 Timothy 6:10 in your Bible.) When people begin to love money, terrible things happen in their soul.

Many of the great heroes of the Bible and down through world history have been people of wealth. Abraham, King David, Solomon, Job, and most of our nation's Founding Fathers were wealthy. The woman considered to be the ideal woman in Proverbs 31 was a woman who knew how to turn a profit and manage her money well.

Wealth is not evil. People who are wealthy aren't evil by virtue of their wealth. There are rich jerks and poor jerks . . . evil rich people and evil poor people . . . spiritually whole rich people and spiritually whole poor people . . . there are both poor and rich people who are obsessed with money and have no thought of God . . . and there are both poor and rich people who are obsessed with obeying God and give little thought to how much their portfolios are worth on any given day.

What About You?

Money causes a person to look in the mirror. I trust that when you do, you truly like the person you see.

Exercise #75

Danger Signals

In the previous exercise, you noted the qualities you want to develop in your life and in your children. Now get REALLY honest with yourself.

What do you see as the potential dangers of your having great wealth? What is the foremost way you believe wealth MIGHT be damaging to your character, your reputation, your integrity, or your relationships? What is it you believe you may have to "guard against"?

_____

_____

_____

_____

_____

_____

Exercise #76

Thoughts to Ponder

Complete as many of the sentences below as possible before consulting the Word Pool. And then . . . ponder these truths!

1. According to Dallas Willard in *Spirit of the Disciplines*, to _____ riches is to cause them to be consumed.

2. According to Willard's book *Spirit of the Disciplines*, to _____ in riches is to count on them for things they cannot provide.

3. According to Willard's book *Spirit of the Disciplines*, to _____ riches is to have the right to say how they will or will not be used.

4. If you are a Christian, it is your spiritual duty to posses riches so you can do with them things that bring glory to _____ .

5. If wealth is spiritually bad, then _____ people can't have it and only bad people get it.

6. It is the _____ of good people to keep wealth from bad people.

7. Wealth is not the _____ to life's questions.

8. If you are a Christian, it is your spiritual duty to possess riches for the good of _____ .

Simple Q & A

Q: According to the American Bankruptcy Institute, more than 1,300,000 bankruptcies are filed each year; _____ percent of these are PERSONAL bankruptcies.

A: 97

9. Perhaps the foremost problem of having money is the tendency to _____ money and to _____ it as a god.

10. If you follow the principles presented in *The Total Money Makeover,* you will either make your life over or end up miserable—it is the _____ aspect of your life that is the vitally important aspect.

Word Pool

God • mankind • answer • worship • duty
use • spiritual • possess • love • trust • good

Answers:

1. use

2. trust

3. possess

4. God

5. good

6. duty

7. answer

8. mankind

9. love; worship

10. spiritual

I encourage you to go back and read aloud each of the above statements with the correct words in the blanks, and then say a hearty "Amen!"

About the Author

After suffering a personal financial loss of a 4 million dollar real estate portfolio, Dave Ramsey decided to return to the basics of personal finance and help others. Dave is the author of the New York Times best-selling book *Financial Peace*. He is also the host of the nationally syndicated *The Dave Ramsey Show*. Many national corporations as well as tens of thousands of individuals have benefited from his Financial Peace University Program and his live seminars. He and his wife, Sharon ("The Princess"), have three children, Denise, Rachel, and Daniel.

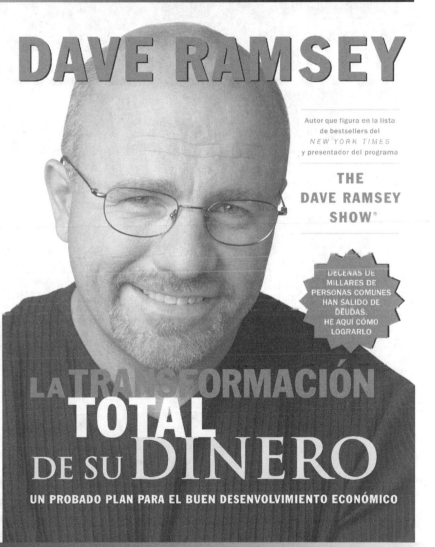